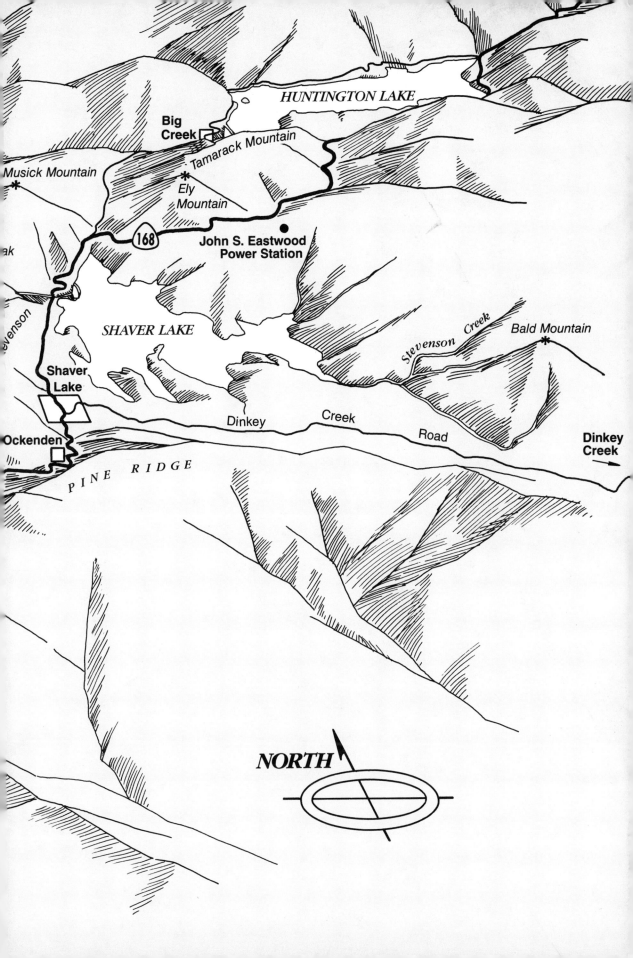

Reflections of Shaver Lake

Reflections of

SHAVER LAKE

Center of activities on Pine Ridge
for more than one hundred years

By
Gene Rose

Word
Dancer
Press

Fresno, California

Library of Congress Catalog Card Number 87-061733
ISBN 1-884995-04-7

Published by Word Dancer Press
Fresno, California

Manufactured in the United States of America

Introduction

On the western slope of California's majestic Sierra Nevada, midway between the towering crest and the valley below, and within the vast San Joaquin River drainage, lies the mountain community of Shaver Lake.

Located fifty-five miles northeast of Fresno at an elevation of 5,300 feet, Shaver Lake has seen vast change during its comparatively short human history. And though its roots are short, its waters run deep, sustaining a dynamic and diversified past.

Ernestine Winchell, the late, highly respected Fresno County historian, once remarked that no location in Fresno County had a more varied human history than Pine Ridge, the general region that now embraces the Shaver Lake basin.

A little more than a century ago, this sprawling mountain ridge was part of a vast wilderness. It was a primitive land, known only to the Indians, who shared the mountains and their meadows with distant cousins across the mountains to the east.

Starting with the first wave of white settlers, who came looking for traces of gold, Shaver Lake has had a rich and colorful history. The early loggers were the first to enter the scene, and the sawmills, in turn, helped set the foundations for the farms and ranches below, enabling Fresno County to grow into the nation's number one agriculture county—a symbiotic relationship that continues to this day.

Down the years, Shaver Lake has known good times as well as bad. It has seen wind, rain and snow. Wildfires and freeze-outs were no strangers either. But Shaver has continued to beckon those looking for recreation, retirement or a new life. In its short stay in the sun, Shaver Lake has hosted a continuing parade of pioneers—those individuals who have been nurtured and sustained by Shaver Lake's special spirit.

This is not an academic history; rather, it is a personal journey back through the woods and world of yesteryear, where the ghosts of the pioneers came forth. Along the way I saw Indians, miners, cattlemen and loggers—dreamers all—seeking a better life for themselves and their families. Enroute, I heard echoes of the past and sounds of the future.

This book is also the stories of those wonderful old-timers who lived in and loved the Shaver Lake area. It is my hope that it will lead to a better appreciation and understanding of the sacrifice those early pioneers made. May it not mark the end of an era, but a new beginning based on a better understanding of the past.

Come, travel along. Follow the forgotten wagon trails, where once the teamster toiled. Explore the old skidways. Seek out the silenced sawmills and the long-gone railroads. Follow in the wake of the old flume. Hitch your buggy to the past and step back into those rich and rugged days of yesterday. I hope you enjoy the trail.

Gene Rose, 1987

Acknowledgments

This book represents more than the assistance of many friends and pioneers of Shaver Lake: it reflects their love and concern for this mountain mecca and the contribution it has made on their lives.

Of the many persons who have contributed either information or photographs, I am especially grateful for the generous assistance from Lewella Forkner of Fresno and Elzy Benson of Fowler. Both of these ninety-plus-year-olds sustain the adage that history is best told by those who have known it firsthand. Forkner arrived in 1892, when her father set the foundation for the huge sawmill that would put Shaver Lake on the map. Benson followed a decade later, making the three-day trip from the valley to the millpond by horse drawn wagon. (The fishing was good then, but not as good as he found it eighty years later.)

I am also grateful to the subsequent pioneers who offered their memories and silver images. John and Velma Harshman were especially helpful, recalling their efforts to set their roots at Shaver Lake in the early 1930s. Ed Steen, an early Forest Service guard, provided additional background. Earlier interviews with Elsie and Charlie Eckhart, now deceased, also helped.

Others who added substantially to this effort include Robert Bretz, grandson of early logger Joseph E. Bretz; Morgan and Knox Blasingame, grandsons of Jesse A. Blasingame, one of the early cattle ranchers; Alice "Tyke" Carleton, grandniece of Tom Ockenden, pioneer Pine Ridge entrepreneur.

As an agency, the U.S. Forest Service was particularly helpful. June English, historian for the Pineridge district, filled in many of the mountainous gaps. Anne Dellavalle located the route of the old flume; archaeologists Larry Swan and Kathy Moffatt—who has since left the agency—came up with a forest of information, particularly on the Indians.

Larry Shannon, Shaver Lake's enduring fire chief, pointed out the old railbed—as well as another perpetual fixture of the early logging camps, the familiar house of ill-fame. William Myers of the Southern California Edison Company, also opened his vast files. The staffs of the Fresno City and County Historical Society and the Fresno Bee editorial library provided valuable assistance also. John Armstrong, Glenn Burns, Isabel Baird, Frank Humphreys, Doug McDonald, Georgia Walsh and Hubert Nevins, all with long ties to the Shaver Lake area, shared their interest and images as well.

The Clovis-Dry Creek Historical Society and the Metro Store of the Fresno Metropolitan Museum of Art, History and Science provided additional help.

Other photographs or assistance came from William Bill Mortland, Jr., John Halverty, Willis Good, Lois W. Steinhauer, Jessie Burnham Hackett and Charlie Hull.

To Bobbye Temple, friend, coworker and copy editor—the grand lady of local history—goes my sincere appreciation.

A special note of thanks goes to Ray Coats of the Shaver Lake branch of the Clovis Community Bank. Without his encouragement—and needling—this book would not have seen print.

Photo Credits

Author's collection, jacket back, 5, 22, 34, 47, 52, 58,
  64, 65, 67, 82, 90, 93
John Armstrong, 43, 46, 64, 78
Isabel Baird, 26
Robert Bretz, 8, 10, 14, 15, 64, 98-99
Knox Blasingame, 21
Alice Tyke Carleton, 74, 75
Lewella Swift Forkner, 3, 12, 30, 31, 36, 44, 48
Fresno Bee, 44 (map), 76 (sketch, Debbie Soligian), 91,
  102, 103, 117
Fresno City and County Historical Society, 9, 89
Willis Good, 89
William Lehr, 8
Henry Halverty, 40, 58
John Harshman, 59, 101, 112, 114, 116
William F. Mortland, Jr., 9, 11, 13, 21, 24, 25, 32, 36, 40,
  41, 45, 53, 57, 83, 107
Doug McDonald, 34, 38, 49, 56, 63, 68, 69, 85, 110
Robert Parker, 103, 104, 113
Ed Steen, 111, 115, 116
Southern California Edison Company, jacket cover, 31,
  60, 95, 96-97
U.S. Forest Service, 8, 47, 73, 77
Carrie Burnham Williams, 19, 39, 78, 88, 109

Table of Contents

CHAPTER ONE

The Mountains and the Monos

It was a mountain wilderness that met Lewis P. Swift and his family as their open wagon struggled up the slopes of the Sierra in the spring of 1892.

The two-day trip from the fledgling town of Fresno had been trying as well as tiring, especially the climb up the steep grade above Tollhouse.

The Swift family and their driver had passed the small general store and tavern that marked the little mountain settlement of Pine Ridge. Four long miles beyond stood the Ockenden Ranch, the last outpost of civilization except for the small Musick and Bretz sawmills, which stood hidden in the tall trees beyond. At this juncture, the wagon trail all but disappeared; yet the Swift wagon continued, the driver picking the way between the trees, dodging large boulders and skirting the still soggy meadows.

Although the entire mountain ridge bore the name of Pine Ridge, the land lay crudely mapped, a rugged frontier of still unknown dimensions. Lewis Swift had been here before, a year earlier, accompanied by his business associate Charles B. Shaver. But for his forty-one-year-old wife, Ella French Swift—with two young daughters in hand—each additional turn produced only more concern. Three miles beyond, not far from a place known as Stevenson Meadow, the driver finally halted the horses in front of a small cabin and the family stepped down to survey their wilderness home.

"The cabin was a small, two-room structure, built out of rough lumber, without any lights, running water or any other conveniences," explained Lewella Swift Forkner, some ninety years later.

"For my mother, it was some kind of cultural shock; compared to the fine homes she had known in Michigan, this was the most primitive of conditions.

"There was no Shaver Lake at that time—nothing. My mother saw it as the wilderness of the Wild West—which it was."

But amid the privation of that wilderness, Ella French Swift began setting up house, while her husband set the foundation for the largest sawmill ever to cut its way into Fresno County's history.

The Swifts were not the first to venture onto what would one day become the Shaver Lake landscape. For centuries, the Indians had migrated up and down the mountainside, using the nearby meadows as camping sites in their summer travels across the Sierra.

The genesis of Shaver Lake's human history represents but one second of its mind-boggling geological history.

Long before there were such landmarks as Shaver Lake, the San Joaquin River or the Sierra, there was the land and the sea, with much of the continent lying below the seas. Then millions of years ago, geologists explain, pressures within the earth's core began forcing up certain areas—sections which were to form the dominant features of the land. Volcanoes and earthquakes followed; dinosaurs entered and then exited mysteriously. The Ice Age arrived, ushering in the great glaciers with their massive touch, and the land was changed again.

The evolution of the land mass known as the Sierra Nevada represents a complex sequence of events. Once the major land forms were in place, the weather went to work, carving here and polishing there, bringing change without end. But it was time and more time—the master sculptor—that formed the land, molding the mountains, meadows and valleys.

How and when the first inhabitants, the first Indians, came to the land is not known. Many archaeologists subscribe to the theory that the Indians migrated to North America from Mongolia via the Bering Strait some 18,000 to 20,000 years ago. Down the centuries, their descendants moved slowly southward, spreading out as they went. That migration came not as a single movement, but as a series of steps—marked by the creation of several distinct Indian families. Their arrival in the central Sierra appears to be comparatively recent, perhaps 7,000 years ago.

About that time, a group of Owens Valley Indians, northern Paiutes—whose predecessors had made their way across the Great Basin—climbed to the crest of the Sierra and looked to the west. They apparently liked what they saw; eventually a few continued on down the western slope, following the tributaries of a vast river system. At the lower elevations, they discovered a more bountiful land with a better climate than their eastern slope home.

Anthropologists believe that some of the tribe stayed on. Eventually they emerged as a new tribe—the western Mono. Here along the upper San Joaquin River—they called it the "Shin-Wog-a-nea"—the Monos found a life of comparative abundance. Deer and small game abounded, fish could be seined from the river, acorns, berries and other foods also were plentiful.

Indian women gather in front of the general store at the Shaver sawmill during the 1890s. Their menfolk often worked in the woods or fired the boilers of the huge sawmill.

Simple shelters, small wickiups, were fashioned readily from slabs of tree bark.

A complete picture of early Mono life does not exist, but they apparently led a simple life; their needs and wants were comparatively few. Undoubtedly, they had their lore and legends, as did most other Indian tribes of that age.

The Monos did not forget their cousins to the east. Every summer, once the snow had melted from the high passes, and as their foothill rancherias became oppressively hot, the Indians would head for the hills. Here they would spend the summer, camping and trading. The Monos had acorns, berries, dried fish and other foods. They also had shells and other goods they had obtained from their neighboring tribes, the Yokuts of the valley and the tribes of the coastal areas. Besides salt and pine nuts, the eastern slope Sierra Paiutes had obsidian, the volcanic black glass from which arrowheads and cutting tools—two key components of Indian survival—were made.

The Indians crossed the mountains at numerous locations, including

Mammoth, Mono, Paiute and Pine Creek passes. Whether their travels favored one direction is unknown; the accepted wisdom is that both Monos and Paiutes moved to the mountains. Their trails of obsidian chips, midden soils and bedrock mortar holes bear evidence of their travels.

The Indians came and went, living at lower elevations in the winter, returning in the summer to enjoy the streams and meadows of the mountains. Recent U.S. Forest Service archaeological research suggests that both the populations and trade were greater than originally estimated. There is some evidence that there may have been some limited year-round occupancy of the mountain meadow that is today the Shaver Lake basin.

In the early 1800s, word was relayed from friendly tribes to the west that there were strangers in the land: people with white skin. The early Spanish explorers and missionaries were the first to reach the foothills. In 1826, Jedediah S. Smith, the first white man to cross the Sierra, entered the southern San Joaquin Valley and the adjacent foothills to the east. Adventurer and explorer John C. Fremont, one of the giants of early California history, made a reconnaissance of the unmapped wilderness between the San Joaquin and Kings river drainages in 1845.

These initial contacts did not alarm the Indians as they were short, friendly visits and posed no serious threat to their way of life. But within a year following the discovery of gold at Sutter's Mill in 1848, hundreds of miners moved through the Mother Lode area of the Sierra, disrupting life for all the foothill tribes. The miners claimed Indians' land, shot their game, murdered their families and infected them with diseases for which they had no resistance. When the Indians tried to fight back, they were quickly overwhelmed.

Against this background, known as "The Indian Troubles of 1850," a military fort was established at Fort Miller on the San Joaquin River, providing the miners and early settlers a measure of protection—and a foundation for future developments.

At that time, many of the gold-bearing areas of the Mother Lode were still undiscovered, prompting the Forty-niners to range far and wide of the major mining camps. It was the same story in the foothills of the southern Sierra, with the miners pushing their picks and pans all the way to the Kern River Canyon. Along the San Joaquin River drainage, their efforts left such interesting names as Kaiser Ridge, Coarsegold and Finegold—place names on the crude but emerging map of discovery and disappointment.

The Indians using Piute Pass came through Humphreys Basin and then

Mono Indians spent the winters in their permanent camps in the foothills below today's Shaver Lake. But with the first heat of summer they migrated over much of the western slope of the Sierra, spending the season at Mono Hot Springs and other high country retreats.

down Piute and French canyons—stopping at the popular hot springs at Blayney Meadows and Mono Hot Springs. From there they continued, over Kaiser Pass to where Huntington and Shaver lakes lie today, occupying the land around Auberry and North Fork during the wet months.

"The Indians knew both the upper and lower hot springs and used them for bathing and to cure their various aches and pains," Dr. Earl Coleman of Fresno State College wrote in 1959.

"There are several of their campsites, well defined, around the meadows. No one knows when they first crossed the mountains, but their last journeys appear to have been made about 1920."

Decimated by disease, denied their traditional hunting and gathering lands, their numbers declined. The few surviving Monos were then crowded into Indian rancherias near North Fork or along the base of Pine Ridge. Some of the men managed to find work in the mining camps; others were hired to haul the rough-cut lumber down the mountainside on their backs— on trails cut by their forefathers. Later, others helped build the original Tollhouse Road, and when that was done, they then went to work in the woods or at the sawmills.

"The Indian men worked in the woods as choppers or 'swampers,' limbing the downed trees, or at the sawmill, where they would keep the fire going under the big boilers," recalled Lewella Swift Forkner.

"Their women started coming up to the general store at the mill, where they would buy 'chuck-plow,' their word for 'flour.' They were dressed pitifully, and their little babies were in even worse condition. How they stood the cold I don't know. My mother used to give them clothes, so they would have some protection," she explained.

CHAPTER TWO

Pine Ridge Pioneers

When the first miners arrived in the gold fields of California in the late 1840s, they soon discovered that their tents and crude hovels were poor substitutes for the homes they had known, but lumber for building shelters was in short supply. Unless a miner was skilled with an ax and could hew timber by hand, it was almost impossible to build any kind of a shelter—or the vital sluice box.

Those who abandoned the gold fields soon realized that they also needed lumber—for barns, fences and homes. The first merchants had difficulty obtaining lumber to build their stores, forcing many to use stone for construction. Some of those stone buildings still stand. The only available lumber had to be imported from the Pacific Northwest, and freighted in at great expense by way of San Francisco and Stockton.

Yet when the pioneers at Fort Miller looked to the east, they could see vast stands of trees on the distant ridges. The trees were just standing there, waiting for some enterprising businessman to come along and turn them into lumber—little wonder the pioneers called it Pine Ridge, or the "Pinery."

As early as 1853, Henry Chambers, along with two other residents of the fort, had forced his way up the ridge to cut roofing shakes, ignoring warnings of possible Indian attacks, the pressing need for lumber forcing the issue. A year later, James Hultz set up the first sawmill at Corlew Meadows—now known as Meadow Lakes—and began cutting lumber, using a crude up-and-down mill powered by steam. The story goes that Hultz was a gambler—as were many early loggers—and had recurring bouts with "pokeritis." He subsequently lost the mill in a friendly but costly game to Alexander Hall. Hall's luck ran out three years later when a fire—another recurring occupational hazard that plagued timber operators—destroyed the mill.

But the first cut into the wilderness forest had been made. The boom that followed the gold rush was marked by the arrival of other small sawmills up

John Humphreys

James Hultz

Joseph Bretz

*Pioneer timber operators of Pine Ridge: James Hultz built—and gambled away—
the first Fresno County sawmill, 1854, located near today's Meadow Lakes. John
Humphreys opened the way for Pine Ridge logging by finishing the toll road and
building the first major sawmill in the 1860s. Joseph Bretz arrived in the mid-1870s,
and his descendants continued in the business for another seventy years.*

A mixed team of mules and horses haul logs to John Humphreys' 1888 sawmill. During his working years on Pine Ridge, 1867-1912, the venerable logger ran ten different sawmills—sometimes in partnerships—harvesting over 60 million board feet of timber.

and down the western flank of the Sierra. In 1856, as Fresno County was organized with Millerton as the county seat, the need for lumber increased substantially. A decade later, professional hunters J. H. and J. N. Woods came along looking for deer and bear meat. When the brothers saw the tall trees, they turned their sights to cutting roofing shakes at a small mill atop the Tollhouse grade. They soon discovered that it was easier to cut shakes than it was to get them down the steep, unroaded mountainside. Even though they hired Indians to haul the bundles down the mountainside on their backs, they soon realized that the only practical approach was a wagon road.

In the ensuing weeks, the Woodses hiked the hills above today's Toll-house, looking for a suitable wagon route up the mountainside. Once satisfied, they applied to the county for a franchise to build and maintain a toll road from Big Dry Creek canyon to the top of the ridge. Toll roads, they knew, had been used elsewhere as a way of getting around the initial costs of road-building.

News of their proposed road spread rapidly. One of those who heard of their proposal was John W. Humphreys, the operator of a sawmill near the Mariposa gold diggings. After inspecting the Pine Ridge timber stands and the proposed toll road, Humphreys returned home in the fall of 1866 and laid out plans to move his mill to the pine-covered ridge of eastern Fresno County.

The move was a difficult one, however. After weeks of effort, Humphreys

Oxen were used to skid logs to the early mills, which were moved often to be closer to the timber supply. Man and beast are shown at the Sage shingle and tray mill in 1890.

If the falling of a big pine coincided with the arrival of the traveling photographer, everyone seemed to come out of the wood works. Bretz mill workers and their families line up in 1899 beside a big sugar pine.

Steam-powered donkey engines, dangerous and demanding as they were, provided mechanical muscle for the Sierra loggers. Despite explosions and decapitations—from breaking wire cables—the donkey engine enabled the early loggers to harvest huge volumes of timber.

finally managed to move his equipment and workers to the foot of the mountain, only to discover that the toll road was stalled. After several frustrating weeks of waiting, Humphreys stepped into the void and began pushing construction himself. He hired Indians and Chinese workers from the nearby rancheria and mining camps near Millerton. Finally, after three months of backbreaking labor, they succeeded in pushing a crude road up the hillside, to a point near today's Cressman's.

Meanwhile, at a location about four miles above—now known as the Shaver Ranch—Humphreys' sawyer and millwright, Moses Mock, had cleared a four-acre site and set the foundation for the sawmill. In May of 1867, a steam boiler and other mill equipment were hauled up to the end of the road. From there, a span of eight oxen skidded the equipment to the mill site. By any measure of the times, it was a giant step forward.

Families of Humphreys' workers soon followed, their women led by Martha Humphreys. Here in the wildness of the frontier, they set up camp, constructing crude shelters from sections of cedar bark, similar to Indian wickiups. The mill crew worked and slept in the open, living under the

Almost every phase of early logging was done by man-, mule- or horse-power, as evident in this 1882 loading scene on Pine Ridge. Steam-powered donkey engines, with chute logging, brought some measure of mechanical muscle, but logging remained a back-breaking job for years.

most primitive conditions. By October, the first loads of lumber were moving from the mountainside to waiting customers.

It is difficult to measure the courage and fortitude these pioneers possessed in the face of privation and adversity. Fresno County's premier early-day historian, Ernestine Winchell, wrote: "Here in August 1868, welcomed by screaming saw and clanking log chain, arrived little Mattie, the third child of Mr. and Mrs. John Humphreys—the first white baby born of Pine Ridge."

Life in the woods was severe and harsh. Shortly after the infant's arrival, a severe thunderstorm deluged the sawmill camp. The mother and her baby—along with everything else—were soaked by the downpour—a chilling baptism to the wilderness.

The Humphreys' mill operated at this location until the fall of 1872, cutting 7 million board feet of timber from 300 surrounding acres. The lumber was quickly sold in the valley, where it went into the emerging farms and homes.

In the spring of 1873, as the nearby trees were all cut, Humphreys and Mock were forced to move their mill higher up the mountainside, the first of many such moves in the name of progress.

Bert Hurt, in *A Sawmill History of the Sierra National Forest, 1852-1940*, notes that some of these moves were made independently, while others were in partnership with other operators. Each move was accompanied by bigger saws and larger and larger harvests—often marked by the "cut-and-run" logging practices of the day.

Wood for raisin trays and fruit boxes dries in the Bretz mill yard. Down the years, the availability of Sierra wood products pushed California's lead in agribusiness.

The Humphreys-Mock operation spurred other entrepreneurs to seek their fortunes harvesting the tall trees of Pine Ridge. In 1874, Gus Bering arrived and set up a steam-driven, double, circular sawmill that could cut 20,000 board feet a day—an unheard volume for the time. In two years, his mill cut 3.5 million board feet. Yet Bering's major contribution to the area came not from his ability to cut trees. In 1875, recognizing the need for supplies for the growing numbers of people on the ridge, he set up the area's first general store, near the site of the vacated Humphreys' mill. In the following years a livery, saloon, post office and other services were added, making Pine Ridge a popular and welcomed stop.

In 1881, Moses Mock, working independently, built his first double circular mill on Rush Creek, which he operated for four years before selling to John Smythe and James McCardle in 1885. According to Hurt, this was one of the better sawmills on Pine Ridge. Herman Peterson, who would emerge as a leading Pine Ridge logger, operated it next until the fall of 1912, when the surrounding area was cut out. During those thirty years, the mill cut 60 million board feet of lumber and logged over 2,000 acres.

Other mills came and cut, further enhancing Pine Ridge's reputation as one of California's prime timberlands. The sawmill with the longest operating history belonged to the Bretz family, an operation which spanned three generations and thousands of trees. Sometime in the late 1870s, Joseph S. Bretz arrived on Pine Ridge from his native Iowa and began cutting, never anticipating his descendants would continue to harvest trees for the next seventy years. Whereas many of the mills were cutting lumber, the Bretz mill

A one-log-load en route to the Prescott mill, 1916-1923, one of nearly seventy sawmills which operated in the Pine Ridge area up to World War II. Sawlogs this size have all but disappeared from today's logging scene—as have the solid-tired trucks and the rugged individuals who drove them.

Well into the 1920s—even with the arrival of trucks—logging remained a labor intensive task. Here "bolts" are trucked to a Bretz sawmill, where they were cut into "shook" for raisin trays.

Logs fall into the millpond during 1930s logging operations at the Bretz sawmill, one of three mill-sites the family used during its three-generation stay around Shaver Lake.

gradually changed over to producing vertical-grained bolts, shakes for roofing materials and, eventually, "shook" for raisin trays.

"The Bretz mill cut a little bit of everything, including lumber and shingle bolts, but most of our efforts went into shook for raisin trays," explained Robert Bretz, grandson of the founding mill operator.

"As a young boy, I spent many hours stacking shook, interleaving them so they would dry flat. Once they had dried we would bundle them up and send them to tray factories in the valley."

Yesterday's logging scene was light years away from today's woods operations. For starters, there were no machines, no chain saws or front-loaders; it was muscle power all the way. The trees were felled by hand after the undercut had been made with axes. Then long, two-man crosscut saws made the backcuts. Once down, the trees were limbed, then "bucked" or cut into comparatively short lengths so they could be handled by man-and-mule power. These sections were skidded by oxen—then mules and horses—to the mill, which, out of necessity, was usually located not far away. For longer hauls, the logs were muscled onto crude wooden-wheeled carts. Later on, steam-powered donkey engines and cable skidways came onto the scene, increasing the efficiency of the harvest.

Logging operations followed the seasons; the loggers and mill workers arrived as soon as the snows melted, and they departed when the white stuff reappeared in the fall. The work was difficult and dangerous. Accident and death were part of the job.

In 1883, Hurt recalled, three workers were killed at the Bennett mill in one season. "One man fell into the saws at the mill, another was killed in the woods, and Bennett's brother was killed when a boiler blew up at the mill."

There was little protection for either the loggers or the millworkers. The hours were long and the wages were low, and the mill operators often sought out the young and those down on their luck. As a teen-age mill worker at Dinkey Creek, Elzy Benson watched as a fellow worker was decapitated by a steel cable on a donkey engine.

"I was making fifty cents a day as a water boy for the donkey engine, when one of the crew quit. They offered me the job at one dollar a day, and I worked at it for one day until that fellow was killed. That did it for me, and I got out of there," Benson recalled.

As the number of mills mushroomed, the timber operators were forced to push the operations farther into the mountains. In the 1880s, the government began to take control of the public forest lands, ending the era of free timber. Down the years the number of sawmills declined. Today, most of the big trees and mills are gone; Fresno County is down to one major sawmill. Now, the second- and third-growth logs go down the hill on giant eighteen-wheelers, with 80,000-pound loads—and at speed the old mule skinners never knew existed. Along the way they pass road signs and place names that recall those pioneer woodsmen, giants such as Humphreys, Bretz, Musick, Petersen, Prescott, Ockenden, Littlefield and Yancey—monuments and markers of the real-life Paul Bunyans of Pine Ridge.

Although logging and lumbering never enjoyed the glamour or glitter of gold mining, they supplied some of the important needs of San Joaquin Valley agriculture and contributed substantially to its subsequent wealth. The need for houses, barns, fences, raisin trays and fruit boxes created a marriage that enabled Fresno County to emerge as the nation's number one agricultural county.

CHAPTER THREE

Pioneers and Place Names

About the time John Humphreys and Moses Mock were setting their sawmill in place, an enigmatic individual by the name of William Stephenson moved up the Pine Ridge mountainside for another reason. Having arrived in the San Joaquin Valley from Tennessee as a teen-ager in 1853, Stephenson married in 1866 and settled down as a cattle rancher north of Fancher Creek.

In the years following the gold rush and the Civil War, large herds of cattle and sheep were brought into the wilderness of the San Joaquin Valley to feed an ever expanding population.

No record exists of how Stephenson came to learn of Pine Ridge and its lush meadows, but in the summer of 1867, faced by drought conditions in the valley, he drove a small herd of cattle up the new toll road, looking for green pastures. Some distance above the Humphreys mill, Stephenson came to a large basin, deep in grass and laced by a network of sparkling streams. It was an ideal spot; while his herd grazed nearby, he built a small cabin and began making plans to return the following year.

A handful of other miners and hunters had also come this way, looking for game or gold. In time, they came to refer to the spot as Stephenson's: his meadow, his creek—just a mile or so east of Stephenson's mountain. Somewhere along the way, his incorrectly spelled name was placed on a map or early document; today we know this landmark pioneer as "Stevenson."

Forest Service records credit Stephenson as the first person to bring cattle to the mountains above Pine Ridge, although two sheepmen—identified only as McCrea and Darby—had apparently grazed sheep in the mountain meadows even earlier. Yet it was to Stephenson's credit that he was among the first to see the salvation that the mountain meadows could provide to the drought stressed livestock from the valley below.

Through the years, Stephenson and his wife had ten children, all of whom died before they were thirty. As the surrounding area developed, Stephenson became the first butcher, supplying the logging and cow camps.

In 1891, he sold his 2,300-acre ranch to the Fresno Flume and Irrigation Company for $19,000—a mountainous sum in those days—and retired to his Watts Valley home. He died in 1893.

By then other names had been placed upon the land around Pine Ridge. Elias Wood Pittman, formerly of Louisana, arrived not long after Stephenson, having settled earlier at the bustling town of Academy. Pittman was a professional hunter, working the mountains above Stephenson's mountain ranch, providing deer and bear meat to the mining and logging camps. Somehow, his name was misspelled also, as "Pitman," when it was given to the mountain stream in the area.

Over at Laurel and Dinkey creeks, and up on Kaiser Ridge, a few miners still clung to their golden but fleeting dreams. Others followed, searching for trees or feed. The sheepmen, led by such giants as William Helm, would lay claim to many meadows, setting the stage for future confrontations with competing cattlemen.

In the 1870s also, the Musick family, led by J. J. Musick and his sons, Charles and Henry, moved up from Dry Creek, ranching at first, but eventually turning to logging in the early 1880s. They, along with cattleman John Markwood, also gained some lasting identity as their names were placed on the emerging map of eastern Fresno County; mountains and meadows were their calling cards.

The 1870s were difficult years throughout California, marked by the winter of 1876-77, when the expected rainfall failed to materialize. Without the rains or runoff from the mountains, the long dry summers created conditions unfavorable for ranching or farming. By spring of 1877, Millerton, which usually received fifteen inches of rain, had but two inches. The range grasses shriveled and died. By July, livestock were dying by the thousands. Without reservoirs or irrigation systems, the situation became desperate. History would look back on that drought as one of the worst ever to hit the Golden State—worse than any of the dry years that would follow during the next hundred years.

Today, the severity of the 1877 drought emerges with such place names as Seventy-seven Corral and Sheep's Crossing—harkening back to the drought year when the livestock from the San Joaquin Valley found salvation in the mountains.

One of the ranchers caught up in the drought was Jesse Augustus Blasingame, a veteran of the Mexican War of 1848, who would go on to become one of the cattle kings of Fresno County. A native of Alabama,

The cabin of William Stephenson, pioneer cattleman and butcher, was the first known structure in today's Shaver Lake area, dating back to 1868. His misspelled name, "Stevenson," serves as a place name today, marking a meadow, a mountain and a creek.

Blasingame had come to California near the end of the Civil War, settling just south of Millerton.

Raising sheep at first, but eventually switching to cattle, Blasingame's spread covered nearly 25,000 acres. But at the height of the 1877 drought, even those acres were not enough to offset the devastation. In desperation, Blasingame and other ranchers concluded that their only hope rested in mountain meadows, where the green grass and a few struggling streams gave some hope.

"The drought of 1877 was the reason the cattlemen started going to the mountains," explained Morgan Blasingame, grandson of the pioneer stockman. "A few sheep and cattlemen had been going earlier, but in 1877 conditions were so desperate that you either moved your cattle to the mountains or they died. It was the only way the catteman could survive. There was no supplemental feed then—no permanent pastures."

From the Blasingame ranch, the cattle were driven to the bottom of the Tollhouse grade the first day. On the second day the cowboys started early, pushing the herd up the toll road. It was imperative to get the cattle up the steep grade before the afternoon heat became unbearable; otherwise the rough road might be more than the young calves or big bulls could take. From there it was another two days to Markwood Meadows, the stockmen's gathering spot.

Following a day's rest there, the animals were then moved to any one of a dozen higher ranges—places like Weldon's cow camp, Sample Meadow or Simpson Meadow—other place names that have become part of the Sierra's rich and colorful heritage.

What began as a measure of survival subsequently became a way of life, marked by the coming and going of the herds. It was a progression to the mountains, with cattle drives led by the Akers, Weldons, Simpsons, Corlews, Samples, Shippses, Collinses and descendants of the pioneer stockmen.

Over the years, the competition between the sheep and cattle men for the range became intense. Stories of open warfare were heard for years, but many of the old-timers claim such incidents were the exception rather than the rule.

Jack Simpson, a third generation Fresno County cattleman, said most of those disputes were between rival sheepmen, with eastern Sierra ranchers coming onto the west side ranges to "steal grass" from other sheepmen.

Still, the competition over the mountain meadows continued. The sheepmen claimed the mountains were public lands, and were open to all livestock. But in time, and as the Forest Service came onto the scene, the cattlemen gradually won control of the range, establishing a way of life that would pass from one generation to another.

As the ranchers ran larger herds, it became necessary to employ added help. Cowboys were hired on a regular basis and some stayed on for years—even to become family members. Together, the cattlemen created a way of life—and a colorful chapter in the human history of the Sierra. Their work was difficult and demanding, running from sunrise to sunset. The cattle drives to the mountains began in late May or early June—just as the valley and foothill grasses began giving out.

Marvin Lee Rice, 1893-1984, a native of Burrough Valley and a noted writer and artist, rode the Sierra range during the early 1900s and knew the lot of the cowboy firsthand.

The cowboy's work was rough and rugged; the cattle, a cross between mean Mexican cows and Durhams, were even meaner if not aggressive. A stampede was the nightmare of every stockman, Rice wrote.

"In the spring of 1912 we had a stampede at the Shaver Lake corral. As the

Pioneer stockman Jesse Augustus Blasingame, Jr. found salvation in the lush mountain meadows for his drought-stressed cattle.

A cowboy drives cattle up the Tollhouse Road near Pine Ridge during an early 1900 cattle drive. Some of the big drives took days, involving up to a thousand head. Rounding up the animals and getting them down the mountainside in the fall was often a bigger problem.

For years stockmen drove their animals to the lush mountain meadows above Pine Ridge, creating a way of life that sustained not only their herds but the growth and development of the Shaver Lake area.

cattle ran uphill, and it was a bright moonlight night, we lost only three head. We did not worry about them, as they would eventually work back to our summer range. A few nights later the Ray Pryor cattle stampeded from the same corral. They went down hill into the heavy willows along Stevenson Creek. When counted the next morning they were 50 head short," Rice reported.

Ed Steen, who worked with the Forest Service at the Shaver Lake guard station during the 1930s, remembers the big drives.

"We had a holding corral for the cattle near Musick Meadows, and I often had the job of counting the animals to make sure the cattlemen didn't exceed their allotment, which they were inclined to do.

"As I recall, Blasingame had a permit for 700 animals; they were huge affairs, with cattle strung way down the mountainside. They kicked up huge clouds of dust, and you knew they were coming a long time before they got to the point where we had to count them," Steen recalled.

The Weldon family cattle drives covered three generations and a lot of memories, also. In 1939, for example, Walt Weldon touched off a stampede when he knocked over a tin can in the middle of the night, scattering cows all over the countryside.

As the summer progressed, the cattlemen would push their herds farther into the mountains, to the most inaccessible places, in search of feed. With the first snowfall in the fall, the whole process would be reversed. Rounding up the cattle and getting out of the mountains before the snow got too deep often took on the dimensions of a rout, as cowboys scoured the hills for strays, Weldon related.

A handful of ranchers still take their cattle to the meadows above Shaver Lake, but the big cattle drives are gone. Today, the animals are trucked to the mountains or feedlots. At the same time the ranchers face other battles— elements of which are often beyond their control. Low market prices coupled with high operating costs present one major problem. More demand for recreation land and additional government controls are slowly pushing the descendants of these proud pioneers from the meadows around Shaver Lake.

The distant meadows above Shaver Lake became the summer ranges for the early stockmen, such as the Collins' camp, located at Collins meadow—today's Crown Valley. Pioneer sheepman W. W. Shipp, right with pipe, located Blayney Meadows.

Preceding pages: The original community of Pine Ridge had an identity problem. Near the location of the first Humphreys' sawmill, it was also known as Bering's, Kenyon's, Armstrong's and, finally, the Shaver Ranch.

CHAPTER FOUR

Men to Match the Mountains

Despite what geologists might say, it was the likes of the legendary logger Paul Bunyan who created Shaver Lake.

After cutting over much of Michigan in the late 1800s, many early timber operators, including Charles B. Shaver of Grand Rapids and Lewis P. Swift of Cheyboygan, could see that their mills were running out of trees. It was time to move on, they realized.

The two men toured the forest areas of California in early 1891 and returned home, enthusiastic about what they had seen in the Sierra east of Fresno. They went directly to George Long, a Grand Rapids lumber baron, financier and longtime business acquaintance, and laid out their proposal. What Shaver and Swift had in mind was as far out as the West itself.

While smaller mills had been cutting in the area known as Pine Ridge since 1854, they were limited by their ability to get the sawn lumber down the mountainside, harnessed by slow and expensive freight wagons. Shaver and Swift's plan was not original, but it went far beyond any earlier approach; it was also intended to succeed where others had failed.

As early as 1884, other timber operators had considered building a railroad to Pine Ridge, but these plans were dropped once the cost of pushing the line up the Tollhouse cliffs was known. Subsequent efforts by the Pine Ridge Flume and Irrigation Company to deliver lumber and water with a forty-one-mile-long flume ran out of luck and money at about the same time. After building an earthen dam across Stevenson Creek, it was discovered that the U-shaped flume leaked so much water it couldn't even be used to move lumber for its own completion.

After further study, Shaver and Swift became convinced that a properly designed flume would work. Not only would such a conveyance move

Following page: In 1893, workers posed on the face of the rock-filled dam, replacing an earthen structure built by the Pine Ridge Flume and Lumber Company—one that had been swept away by earlier storms. Remnants of the rock dam still reemerge during low waters.

Lewis P. Swift, the real-life Paul Bunyan of Shaver Lake, designed, built and ran the giant sawmill.

While the Lewis P. Swift family "carriage" was little more than a buckboard, it provided some diversion for the sawmill superintendent's family during the initial decade at the Shaver mill. Lower left, Lewis P. Swift and his family relax at their spartan mountain home, a simple structure located near the huge Shaver sawmill. An unidentified nanny holds daughter Gertrude. An elder daughter, Lewella, is at her father's side.

lumber, but the spent water could then be sold to water-hungry ranchers and farmers in the valley.

The Michigan group began to organize. They first secured the rights of the original flume company, which they reorganized under the name of the Fresno Flume and Irrigation Company. Next, they began acquiring the surrounding timberlands, including the Henry and Charles Musick sawmill—for which the brothers received cash and stock. Several smaller mills also were acquired. From William Stephenson, the enigmatic rancher who had come to the mountain meadow twenty-four years earlier, the company purchased another 2,300 acres of timberlands.

For a new flume, the new company turned to John S. Eastwood, a brilliant young engineer who had a private practice outside his job as Fresno's first city engineer. He designed a V-shaped flume—which would have about half the joints and seams of the earlier flume. It would run all the way to the emerging community of Clovis, where a planing and finishing mill would be located. It was a prudent move, events would show.

Not long thereafter, Shaver and Swift, followed by two dozen key employees and their families from their Michigan mills, arrived at the new site. Swift, who had been pouring over plans for months, took over construction of the mill and flume. Shaver spent most of his time in Fresno, applying his talents to the business side of the operation.

The sawmill went up rapidly, built with lumber from the Musick mill. But no sooner had it been completed than disaster struck. A huge storm washed away the existing earthen dam, which was to create the millpond and source of water for the flume. Undaunted, more workers were hired and a new rock-filled dam was constructed in the same area. It was about fifty feet high and 300 feet long—situated almost perpendicularly to the southernmost end of today's concrete dam, 100 feet lower and to the east.

Countless other difficulties plagued the project, located as it was, two or three days away from the nearest source of supply. But within a year the mill was cutting lumber, much of which went into building the new flume.

Swift's older daughter, Lewella, who would grow up to become Mrs. J. C.

Facing page: By 1900, the Shaver sawmill and millpond were at the center of eastern Fresno County commerce, cutting lumber and contributing to the economic development of the mountains and valley. Today's Shaver Lake makes a similar contribution, generating power—and recreation.

The Shaver sawmill, its sights and sounds now gone, once echoed over Pine Ridge, cutting some twenty million board feet a year during its twenty-six-year life. The causeway stood atop the dam, providing access to the sawmill and the community of Shaver. The dam also impounded a 5,000-acre-foot millpond.

Looking from Shaver Point to Bald Mountain—the original Shaver millpond held but a fraction of the storage of the man-made reservoir that came upon the scene in 1927.

Facing page: From mid-November to mid-April the Fresno Flume and Lumber Company's giant Shaver mill stood idle, watched over by a small caretaker crew.

A maze of flumes radiated out from the Shaver sawmill during the heyday of logging in what is today's Shaver Lake basin. The flumes enabled the firm to move sawn lumber down the steep Pine Ridge grade—without the expense and delay that went with the old mule-drawn freight wagons.

Forkner of Fresno, was a young child at the time, but the memory of those early activities remained with her.

"My father spent that first year in planning . . . trying to decide where to put the mill and all the other buildings," Mrs. Forkner recalled.

"We came in 1892; the entire area was called Pine Ridge then, not Shaver Lake or Shaver. My father was the mill superintendent, in charge of construction and operation, while Mr. Shaver was the general business manager, who spent most of his time in Fresno.

"There was nothing there when we arrived; it was true wilderness. My father hurried around to build a small cabin, but it was very primitive living. My mother found it a very difficult life; she saw it as the Wild West."

By any measure, construction of the sawmill, dam and flume were herculean feats, built by real men—with the imagination and pioneering spirit of Paul Bunyan himself.

52 Mill yard

Shaver

Sections of sawlogs dwarf a young logger on the Fresno Flume and Lumber Company's vast holdings near Dinkey Creek. At its peak, the company controlled over 32,000 acres of timberland, serviced by a fifteen-mile-long railroad, sections of which are visible at upper left.

The new flume was built right above the old U-shaped structure. Lumber for extending the flume was floated down the completed sections, expediting construction. In some sections, towering trestles had to be built from the bottom of ninety-foot-deep canyons. In other areas, workmen had to be lowered down sheer rock faces to install the necessary footings.

Everything connected with the project was staggering. The giant boilers and huge saws had to be hauled up the mountainside by freight wagons. Financial problems caused other mountainous difficulties. In 1893, just as the mill was to cut its first lumber, a depression hit the country, further impacting the project.

On more than one occasion, according to Mrs. Forkner, robbers held up the stage coming up to the mill, taking the payroll, further strapping the already cash-short operation. As a result, the company was forced to use payroll vouchers which were redeemable only at the Fresno office—and only if funds were available at the time. Under these conditions some employees had to sell their vouchers for fifty cents on the dollar, aggravating already shaky labor relations. On several occasions, she recalled, workers even threatened her father.

Turn of the twentieth century technology: Sawlogs were brought to the Shaver millpond or railroad by a network of log chutes and endless cables, powered by a steam-driven donkey engine.

In town, Shaver was often forced to hide from creditors. But the company hung on, thanks to the perseverance of both men.

Swift, a native of Indiana, had left home at an early age to make his way in the world. During the Civil War he enlisted in the Union army and served as an officer. After leaving the army, he lived in Illinois and Michigan, where he learned every phase of the lumber business.

A talented man and an ingenious mechanic, Swift could improvise almost anything the mill needed. Instead of ordering expensive new parts and waiting months for their arrival, he often fashioned them out of scrap iron—which earned him the nickname of "Scrap Iron Swift." But more than anything, he was a man with a great vision who could overcome great obstacles to reach his goal.

As the mill developed, a mailing address was needed. The postal service was petitioned for a post office that would be known as Swift, California. However, there were other locations with that name, so the mill site was called "Shaver" in honor of Swift's partner. The appendage "Lake" would be added much later.

The Shaver mill relied on two Shay locomotives that worked spur lines as far away as Dinkey Creek, bringing loads of sawlogs to the millpond. Acquired in 1902 and 1906, the engines were the workhorses of the logging camp, boosting production significantly.

The mill workers lived in a small settlement in the area known as Sulphur Meadows—which consisted of the mill, blacksmith shop, drying kiln, general store, barn, stage shop and a cluster of cabins. A one-room schoolhouse was built later, Mrs. Forkner related.

"My father was very strict. There were no alcohol or single women allowed at the Shaver mill, as there were in some of the other sawmill communities."

The new flume was not completed until June of 1894, representing an expenditure of some $200,000 and 9 million board feet of timber.

Trees for the new mill were felled by hand and hauled to the millpond by way of log skidways and cableways. A little steamer, "Michigan," towed booms of logs to the mill. Here the timber was cut and partially dried—so it wouldn't sink—and was then sent down the flume to Clovis.

Workers known as "flume tenders" were stationed along the route to

Logs brought by rail car were dumped at the far end of the millpond and then towed across to the mill in booms of logs. Excessively wet logs often sank when they hit the water, leaving the bottom of the pond covered with "sinkers."

Mill workers gather around one of the big circular saws which screamed their way through the Shaver mill sawlogs. The workers' life was not an easy one—back-breaking labor, long hours and low pay. The fringe benefits of crowded bunkhouses, a seasonal job and privation were offset only by ample cookhouse food.

Long before the armada of pleasure boats arrived on Shaver Lake, the steamboat "Michigan" was at work. For years the venerable tugboat moved booms of logs across the millpond, from the rail dump at the southeast end of the lake to the mill.

Shaver sawmill workers gather atop a sawlog, following the 1901 conversion from a double-circular saw to a faster, more efficient band or continuous saw.

A large log on a railed saw car approaches the steam-driven saws at the Shaver mill. During its twenty-six years of operation, the giant mill cut 450 million board feet of lumber—the equivalent of enough wood to build a city the size of San Francisco.

prevent jams, and as much as 200,000 board feet of lumber floated down the
waterway every day, a six-and-a-half-hour-trip to the Clovis finishing mill.
On occasion, log jams did occur, causing the water to spill out over the sides
of the flume, washing away the supporting foundations, and, all too often,
the flume itself.

On a few occasions, "flume picnics" were staged for mill workers and
their families, during which the braver ones floated through the slower,
more placid sections of the man-made mountain aqueduct.

Shortly after the project was completed, Shaver, Swift, Ella Swift and Ida
Musick took a ride down the flume. After covering half the distance they
bailed out. "The party was soaked with water and felt quite dizzy," Ida
Musick reported.

The most thrilling part of the flume ride was the steep section between
today's Pine Ridge Elementary School and Tollhouse. Cliff Field of Pine
Ridge remembered the day Shaver missed the stagecoach to the valley and
decided to ride the flume down, figuring he could catch the stage before it
got to Tollhouse.

"Shaver came running into the store and asked my father-in-law, Am-
mond Cressman, for help. He directed Shaver to the place where the flume
crossed 'the saddle'—that point between Jose Basin and Tollhouse valley.
They got into one of the little flume boats and started down.

"Of course it was a thrilling ride. It only took seven minutes to make it
down from the saddle to where Lodge Road is today. He told Shaver to stay
seated, but they got going so fast that Shaver's derby hat flew off. Shaver
stood up to grab it, but my father-in-law grabbed him and managed to pull
him back down; otherwise he would have been thrown out," Field reminisced. Field's story doesn't tell how, or if, Shaver caught up with the stage.

The flume was the subject of other tall tales. Supposedly, the millworkers
used the flume boats to reach the "flesh spots," bars and gambling dens of
Fresno. Once relieved of their hard-earned money, they would head back for
the forest and the mill, by way of a freight wagon or stagecoach.

In spite of the company's successes, however, a major problem developed.
Shaver and Swift had not reckoned on the likes of Henry Miller, the cattle
and land baron. His company, Miller & Lux, along with the San Joaquin &
Kings River Canal Irrigation Company, held the water rights to both rivers.
Just as the lumber company was beginning to make money, it was hit by a
lawsuit over water diversions into the flume. In the ensuing litigation, a
settlement was eventually worked out that granted the company enough

In 1894, workers finished the Shaver-Clovis V-shaped flume, set on top of an earlier U-shaped flume.

water to move its lumber, but prohibited the delivery of irrigation water. The ruling dashed any possibility of irrigation revenues and only brought on additional lawsuits—from those landowners who had granted rights-of-way for the flume in exchange for planned irrigation water.

Despite the problems, the mill survived. At its peak the mill could cut 200,000 board feet a day, with about six hundred workers employed during the mid-April to November milling season.

Mrs. Forkner remembered, "Father would go up in April . . . as soon as the snow melted, and get things ready, and then the workers would come up.

"There were a few families—particularly those who had come out from Michigan—who stayed all year and took care of things. Their lives were not very pleasant, particularly during those long, isolated winter months. Because there were families and children living there all year, my father built a small school and hired a teacher so the children could have some schooling."

Still, it was an exciting time, she recalled.

"During the summer it was a beautiful, enjoyable place. We had all kinds of fun, hiking, picnicking and playing around the mill; the workers really

Route of old Shaver Lake flume

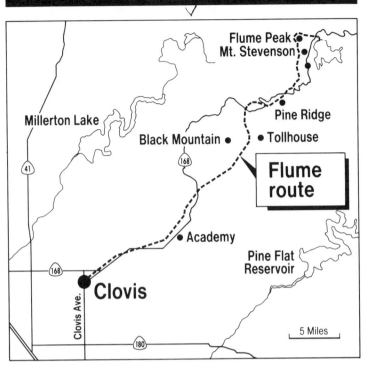

Flume Peak
Mt. Stevenson
Pine Ridge
Millerton Lake
Black Mountain
Tollhouse
168
Flume route
Academy
Pine Flat Reservoir
41
168
Clovis Ave.
Clovis
180
5 Miles

Opposite page: The forty-two mile Shaver-Clovis flume delivered a forest of lumber to the valley for more than twenty years, spurring growth and development in the Fresno-Clovis area. Longer flumes from other Sierra lumber camps terminated at Madera and Sanger, but served fewer years than the Shaver flume.

Rough lumber, partially dried at Shaver kilns, moves down the flume to the Clovis finishing mill. Several people were killed or injured in falls from the narrow walkway, left foreground. The man-made waterway operated for twenty years before it was put out of service by snow slides and storm damage.

Above: A Shaver mill worker dumps lumber into the flume, sending the rough-sawn boards on their way to the Clovis finishing mill. Other mills on Pine Ridge also utilized the man-made waterway under contract.

Above Tollhouse, the flume clung to the steep cliffs. Rough, partially-dried lumber was loaded in the flume before dawn and started on its way, arriving— it was hoped—at Clovis seven hours later.

At twelve sites along the forty-two-mile-long flume, small cabins were established for the "flume-tenders," who maintained the flume and kept the rough-sawn lumber moving toward the Clovis planing mill.

The Shaver-Clovis flume had all kinds of problems—even after it reached the valley floor. Constant leaks weakened the framework; high winds and storms often toppled sections. Flume crews were kept busy repairing the man-made waterway.

Log jams were common along the flume. Flume-tenders were kept busy keeping the lumber moving. Water spilling over the sides often undermined the supporting framework, causing sections to fall.

Rough-sawn lumber speeds down the Shaver flume to the Clovis finishing mill, making the forty-two-mile trip in about six hours. In use from 1894 to 1915, a forest of lumber came down the man-made waterway—as did many sawmill workers en route to the gambling dens and fleshspots of Fresno.

watched out for us, making sure we would not get hurt or into trouble. We didn't do much swimming, but we had a lot of fun around the millpond.

"We even felt sorry for those suffering the heat in Fresno."

Mrs. Forkner said that the camp cookhouse was one of her favorite spots. Six Chinese cooks and their kitchen staff served meals six times a day.

In 1901 tragedy struck. Just as Swift was completing the conversion of the mill to a more efficient circular or continuous saw operation, he was stricken by a heart attack and died at his Fresno home; medical science of the day listed his death as "apoplexy."

Shaver immediately contacted Swift's brother, Harvey, who had remained in Michigan, and asked him to take over. Harvey Swift came to Fresno, purchased his dead brother's interest in the company and took over the responsibilities at the sawmill.

By 1902, the timber near the mill had been harvested and it was difficult to obtain logs, so a railroad was built toward Dinkey Creek. In later years, the line would be extended and a second engine added.

At the "cross-over"—near today's Pine Ridge School—the flume began its steepest descent to the valley below. Rough-sawn lumber from smaller sawmills—mills under contract to the flume company—was launched into the flume for delivery to the Clovis finishing mill.

Shaver died in 1907 and was succeeded as head of the company by Harvey Swift. By the summer of 1911, it was estimated that nearly two thousand persons—loggers, mill workers, merchants and visitors—were in the mill area. A campground—with electricity generated at the mill—had even been established for those seeking relief from the heat of the valley.

In December 1911, Swift suddenly sold his interest in the mill for just under $1 million to Ira Bennett, the former manager of the sawmill at Hume Lake. The new company was named the Fresno Flume & Lumber Company of Nevada; "Irrigation" had been dropped from the name years earlier, following the settlement of the initial Miller & Lux lawsuit.

During the next two years the mill's production boomed, with a daily cut of enough lumber to build twenty-four average-sized houses. However, the new owners were under-capitalized. When a big storm swept away sections of the aging flume, it came as a death blow. A year later the mill was shut down.

In 1919, the sawmill and the company's holdings were purchased as part of the planned extension of the Big Creek hydroelectric project. And while the mill provided timber for construction at Southern California Edison Company's Huntington and Florence lake dams, the mill never again cut to the levels it had known.

In its day, the mill was one of the largest Fresno County had ever known, cutting a total of 450 million board feet of timber—an amount that would have impressed even Paul Bunyan.

CHAPTER FIVE

Charles B. Shaver

Charles Burr Shaver, whose name would be given to the most prominent landmark on Pine Ridge, was born August 7, 1855, in Steuben County, New York, the third of four children born to Mary Rose and John L. Shaver, a miller by trade.

At his birth no one could have foreseen that one day he would leave his mark on a mountain meadow high on the western slope of California's majestic Sierra.

Shaver's rendezvous with destiny took a rather direct course. Some time during the Civil War his family moved to Michigan, where his father turned to farming. Nine years later, when Shaver was eighteen, he began working in the lumber business at Detroit, employed by the firm of Whitney and Stinchfield. Within a year, he was promoted to woods foreman and served in that role for eight years, until 1882, when he joined A. B. Long and Son of Grand Rapids. In the next seven years Shaver came to know every facet of the lumber business, from the forest and mill to the marketplace, acquiring skills and experience that would serve him in later life.

In 1889, Shaver became the general manager of the White and Friant Lumber Company, supervising the construction of a logging railroad that enabled the firm to cut 100 million board feet of lumber in a two-year period—impressive by any measure. Looking around for more standing trees, he turned next to Neelysville, Missouri, where he erected yet another sawmill, in 1891, just prior to his relocation to Fresno and Pine Ridge.

Shaver married Lena A. Roberts of Pennsylvania on December 6, 1883. Of that marriage three daughters were born, Grace, Ethel and Doris, all of whom would one day make their own contribution to Shaver Lake's history.

Shaver was a dynamic individual who had a flair for getting things done. The fact that he could launch a million dollar operation—the Fresno Flume and Irrigation Company—with only $30,000 spoke of his abilities as a salesman.

Charles B. Shaver, right, with his wife, Lena, and daughter, Doris, and Betty Maupin, Ethel Shaver and an unidentified man, in front of Shaver's Fresno home.

Soon after moving to Fresno, Shaver quickly became one of Fresno's foremost citizens, based largely on his company's contribution to the Fresno-Clovis economy. He held membership in a half dozen civic organizations, further establishing his reputation in the growing community.

"Mr. Shaver spent most of his time in Fresno, attending to financial matters and making sure the finished lumber was delivered to the railroad or wherever it had to go," Lewella Swift Forkner recalled.

"As the mill began to cut more lumber, the company established its own telephone line. Every day Mr. Shaver would call up to my father to find out how much lumber they had cut that day, or to discuss any problem that might have developed, such as a mechanical breakdown or labor difficulties."

In town or at the sawmill, Shaver was a familiar figure, easily recognized by his dark suit, stubby cigar and derby hat. "Portly of figure, genial of countenance . . . passionately fond of a good cigar," was how one Fresno newspaper described the lumber magnate.

Charles B. Shaver, 1855-1907, lumber pioneer; a lake became his nameplate for eternity.

At capacity, today Shaver Lake's serpentine shore line affords more than twenty miles of beaches, coves and recreational opportunities, as evident in this aerial photo. Named for Charles B. Shaver, the reservoir also provides power, and additional recreational uses.

For Charles B. Shaver's wife, Lena, their sawmill retreat stood as her preferred home —and not her Fresno mansion. In 1919, to make way for the proposed dam, it was torn down and moved to Rock Haven as the genesis of that mountain subdivision.

Besides cigars, Shaver enjoyed horses and reportedly owned several race-horses. But when horseless carriages began making their appearance, Shaver was at the head of the pack.

"My grandfather had one of the first Stanley Steamers in Fresno. Every morning, after he got it fired up, he would roar through the downtown area . . . for which he acquired the nickname of 'Cannon Ball Shaver,'" reminisced Doug McDonald.

"He used to delight in running up and down the streets, and the noise of the Steamer was warning for those with horses to get their teams off the street."

At work, Shaver had a similar style. He was direct and to the point. The company correspondence contains volumes of five- and six-line letters. His regular communications to his Michigan backers often reflected hope rather than reality. "Things are going well . . ." appeared frequently in those messages.

Lumber, destined for Fresno and other areas of California, rims the Shaver sawmill, around 1903, when the giant mill was at its peak. The Shaver cabin was located in the trees, upper left.

Unfortunately, Shaver was not to share in the financial rewards that accompanied the 1911 sale of the sawmill. Shortly after he turned fifty, a goiter, or carbuncle, formed on the back of his neck, a condition the medical science of the day was unable to treat. Compounded by diabetes, the infection took hold and he gradually weakened. On Christmas Day, 1907, surrounded by his family and four of Fresno's most prominent doctors, Shaver died at his Stanislaus Street mansion.

In his thirty-inch obituary, the *Fresno Morning Republican* eulogized the lumber king of the community:

> In his death the county of Fresno has lost a public-spirited man, a good and honorable citizen and a prominent figure in commercial life.

> The Fresno Flume and Irrigation Co. enterprise was the crowning work of the late C. B. Shaver's life ambition and of his best efforts under circumstances and conditions of finance and commercial depression which would have discouraged many another man. It was under great physical and mental strain under which he labored to bring this enterprise to a successful issue which undermined his once robust

During so-called dry years, the remains of the old rock-filled dam are re-exposed, recalling those early days when Swift and Shaver stood above the pioneering scene. Ely Mountain rises in the background.

Facing page: Caught in a friendly snowball fight, Charles B. Shaver, foreground, scurries for cover during a rare winter visit to the snow-bound sawmill.

Shaver's grandson, Doug McDonald, believes that this unidentified flume rider is none other than Charles B. Shaver, who is known to have made a few frightening rides down sections of the man-made waterway.

health. Sad therefore, that in the prime of life, while enjoying the material fruits of his labor and commercial sagacity, he should be called from this world.

Shaver's funeral at the Fresno Episcopal Church was one of the largest the community had seen. He was buried at Mountain View Cemetery.

Shaver's legacy, among the trees and mountains, would endure, with his name serving as a landmark. His widow, Lena, led a long and active life, spending winters in Fresno and summers at Rock Haven or the Shaver Ranch. She died on May 11, 1939, at age seventy-five, at her Echo Avenue home.

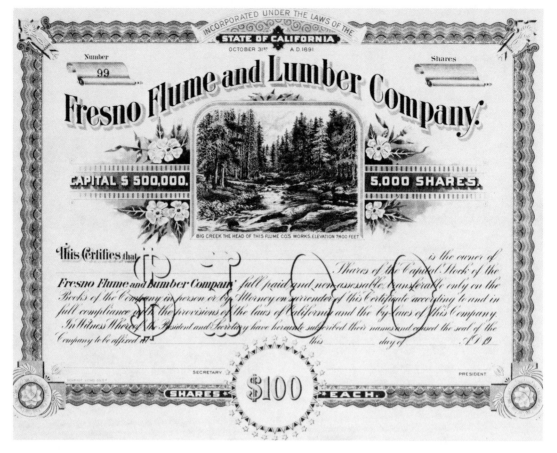

Fresno Flume and Lumber Company stock of October 31, 1891, mysteriously claimed Big Creek waters, which were miles away in another drainage. An accompanying issue, "Fresno Flume and Irrigation Company," poses more unanswered questions.

"My grandmother's real home was in the mountains; they were her first love. She wanted to die up there," McDonald reflected.

In an ironic twist of fate, Shaver's eldest daughter, Grace Craycroft, drowned in 1940—in Shaver Lake—while attempting to save two young boys. The two surviving sisters, Ethel Hoover and Doris McDonald, led full lives.

Today one of C. B. and Lena Shaver's grandchildren, Doug McDonald, occupies the Shaver Ranch property, while his children play in the waters of the lake named after their pioneer great-grandfather.

CHAPTER SIX

Travel and Trauma

Today's Shaver Lake travelers shake their heads in disbelief at the difficulties and delays experienced by those making the same journey a little more than a century ago.

When the first white explorers came into the area known as Pine Ridge, they traveled on foot, following faint trails used by the Indians. Those who followed came on horseback or with a pack mule, gradually pushing a marked trail into the wilderness.

Once the Woods brothers' toll road was in place, the mountain travelers still faced hardships. Ox-drawn wagons and horses and buggies eventually gave way to huge freight wagons, which, in turn, surrendered to the horseless carriage—each in its own way testifying to the ruggedness of yesterday's pioneers.

Almost everything that was to become Shaver Lake was pushed or pulled up the mountainside by horse or mule power: the huge boilers that would power the giant saws, the rails and the locomotive that would become the Shaver Lake Rail Road and all the people and provisions that would make the mill operational came up the hill behind four-legged hayburners.

To sustain the people employed at the Shaver mill, as well as the smaller mills on Pine Ridge, and at all the hotels, liveries and other support businesses along the way—a spring-to-fall community estimated at more than a thousand persons—food and other supplies moved up the mountainside behind horse- or mule-drawn wagons.

Completed in August 1868, the toll road had one of the most murderous grades in the country. It climbed 2,000 feet in less than four miles, with some of the slopes measuring 30 percent. On hot summer days the grade took a terrible toll of draft animals, developing a reputation as a "beast killer."

The toll rates also were considered "killers" by some. For a wagon and span of horses, mules or oxen, the cost was a dollar and a half, plus fifty cents for each additional span. The fee for a horse and buggy was one dollar; a horseman, fifty cents; packed or led animals, twenty-five cents; loose mules, horses or cattle, ten cents a head; and sheep or hogs, two cents a head.

At the height of the freighting era—generally regarded as the turn of the century—upward of sixty freight wagons lumbered up and down the mountainside each week. A typical round trip between Shaver and Fresno—allowing a day for loading and reloading—consumed a week.

While lumber sold for twelve dollars a thousand board feet at the mill, the cost of hauling it down the mountainside ran the price up another thirty dollars a thousand. Until the completion of the Fresno Flume and Lumber Company's man-made waterway, all the mills relied on freight wagons to get the sawn lumber down the steep hillside.

Veteran mountain packer Glenn Burns of Clovis saw the twilight of that teamsters and freight-wagon era. The sight of the great wagons fighting their way up and down the mountainside was something to behold, he recalled.

"They ran up to twenty mules, but most of those running the Tollhouse grade were twelve-mule teams. It was generally figured that one mule could pull one ton, depending on the condition of the road. They hauled lumber down and supplies going back up.

"The teams were controlled by a single jerkline. On the sharp hairpin turns, the mules would have to move sideways, stepping over the main chain so they could round the turns. There were 'leaders, pointers and wheelers,' and the mule skinner had to know each one by name, calling out their name, getting them to move right or left at the right moment to the commands of 'gee' and haw.'"

Undoubtedly the most difficult feat was fighting the big loads down the mountainside, because the wooden brakes of the day were no match for the steep grade. There was one small sawmill on Pine Ridge that cut nothing but wood brake blocks, Burns noted. Even then the wooden brakes were inadequate.

"What they did was to attach a kind of iron sled or skid to the front wheels of the second wagon that was chained to the rear axle of the front wagon . . . so the wagon slid down the road," Burns recalled.

Teamster Joe P. Winkleman is credited with hauling the largest load ever taken down the grade. He had his team so well trained that he could drop the lines and direct the animals by oral commands, including a few undeleted expletives. Like other logging teamsters on the grade, he often tied a tree behind his wagon to act as a brake on the perilous downward trip.

Mule power! The progress and developments at what was to become Shaver Lake were made possible by mule-drawn freight wagons. For years, mule wagons—often eight-, ten- and up to twenty-four-mule teams—forced their way up the steep grades, taking a week to make the round trip to Fresno.

The largest load ever to come up the hill was the Shay locomotive that was used to haul logs into the millpond. Combining his two teams, for a total of twenty-four animals, Alfred M. Starkey performed this feat in the summer of 1906, moving the engine up the hairpin turns of the steep grade.

Starkey was only twenty-six years old when he made his epic haul. He lived a long life; however, many of the Tollhouse teamsters were not so lucky. Wagon wrecks took a terrible toll of lives and limbs. "Accident Hill" and "Deadman's Home" bear further witness to two of the many terrible turns on the grade. "Jacoby's Hill," right above Cressman, was named for a teamster killed along the way.

When one of these wagon teams was heard coming down the grade, the wise traveler gave it full range. It was not uncommon for horse-and-buggy travelers to unhitch their rigs and move their animals off the grade. Then the big lumbering wagons, their brakes squeaking and smoking, could go by, accompanied by the familiar cloud of dust.

Legendary, enigmatic, photographer Robb W. Riggs was one of the first to set up business at the Ockenden Ranch, 1884.

Gus Bering established the first store on Pine Ridge in the early 1870s, providing a measure of progress and a source of supply to the early toll road travelers.

The community of Pine Ridge, located near the site of the original Humphreys' Clipper saw-mill, played a major role in the development of eastern Fresno County. Highway 168 follows the old wagon routes, past today's Shaver Ranch, four miles below Shaver Lake.

When the first wave of tourists or recreation seekers came, they followed in the wagon ruts—and the dust—left by the big wagons.

Elzy Benson of Fowler was a young boy when he made his first trip to the Shaver Lake millpond in July 1903. Out of necessity, it was a ten-day outing, because each leg of the trip took three days—by horse-drawn wagon!

"My father had heard that there was some real good fishing up there, so we got together with another family and planned a Fourth of July trip with them. The first day we managed to get up past Academy at a place known as Bell Station, near Letchers.

"On the second day we got as far as Tollhouse, where we spent the night in an open field right by the wagon. On the morning of the third day, the men got up about 4 A.M. and got the animals harnessed so we could get started the minute it got light—kind of feeling our way up the old toll road.

"Even then, the grade was so steep that everyone had to walk alongside the wagon, and then we had to stop about every twenty minutes and rest the horses. When we did stop, a big block had to be placed behind the rear wheel of the wagon to keep it from rolling backward.

"It was a difficult and demanding trip up the mountainside. There were a couple of springs and watering troughs along the way. On the steeper section the women and children were even required to help push the old Moline wagon up the hillside. By late morning we arrived at Widow Waite's, located on the saddle not far from today's community of Shaver Springs.

"Actually the toughest part was right above Jacoby's Hill. This section of the wagon road was extremely steep and rough."

Late the third day, the tired travelers and the weary wagon team pulled into the Ockenden Ranch, bypassing the hotel to camp in a remote section above the historic resort.

"I can't remember if we slept in the wagon or whether we rolled out our blankets nearby. What I do remember is that it was cold and uncomfortable; we didn't have anything like sleeping bags or any of the conveniences campers have today," Benson reminisced.

What the group did have was a wonderful time. After resting a day, they wagoned over to Shaver sawmill for the Fourth of July celebration. The holiday was marked by the firing of a large cannon at the mill, followed by a picnic and fishing on the millpond.

"We had heard that the fishing was good and it was. Somehow we were able to borrow a rowboat, and we did some trolling and caught several large rainbow trout, a couple of which were over twenty inches in length.

"But we were warned that we would have to soak the fish overnight in fresh stream water to get rid of the taste of the millpond; otherwise the fish would taste like pine trees."

A day later, the Benson party made an overnight trip to Dinkey Creek, where they camped near a small logging mill. On the following day, they journeyed over a rough trail to a grove of giant Sequoias, destined to be known as McKinley Grove.

For the young Benson, it was something akin to exploring the Wild West. In one small tributary, he saw Chinese miners working a sluice box, looking for gold. In another location, loggers were skidding sawlogs to a railroad spur—scenes that have long disappeared from the landscape.

"We camped out every night, cooking over a campfire, using only food we had brought from home. As I recall, there wasn't much variety—bacon, potatoes, bread and coffee. We had some other vegetables at first, but there was no refrigeration or camp coolers in those days.

"Most of the cooking was done in a dutch oven that we put right into the coals of the fire. By comparison with what we had later, it was really primi-

An early passenger stage pauses at the foot of the Tollhouse grade, prior to the arduous climb up the mountainside to Pine Ridge and the Shaver sawmill.

tive, but we never went hungry and we enjoyed it tremendously.

"We just didn't realize it was wilderness camping, no matter how primitive.

"Getting down the Tollhouse grade was tougher than getting up. It was the most dangerous part of the whole trip. At one point, the men had to cut down a fairly good-sized tree and chain it to the back of the wagon to keep it from running away with them."

For many years, he added, the bottom section of the Tollhouse grade was lined with piles of "brake" trees that had been drug down the grade by other cautious travelers.

From 1902 to 1912, W. R. "Billy" Miles and J. R. "Jim" Parish drove freight wagons and then stagecoaches to Shaver Lake. As a young man, Miles had started as a "swamper" before becoming a teamster or mule skinner for the Fresno Flume and Lumber Company, fighting mind-boggling loads up the tortuous grade.

Those great scenes of yesteryear are gone. But for those old-timers, the sight of those great mule teams moving around the mountainside was, indeed, power and poetry in motion.

In 1906 Miles and Parish began hauling passengers. Their stagecoach left Fresno at 4 A.M. and arrived at Shaver Lake at 6 P.M.—fourteen hours of

Early motorists—real adventurers in their day—force their way up the wagon road at Pine Ridge—often using reverse gear to climb the steeper grades. Here, near the Shaver Ranch, today's Highway 168 follows much of the same alignment.

rattling and rolling up the mountainside.

"It was the only passenger traffic between the two places at that time. We used six horses between Fresno and Tollhouse and eight horses from Tollhouse on to Shaver," Miles recalled. "Even then, all the men had to get out and walk while the horses pulled the coaches up the grade."

At the top of the grade, two of the horses would be cut loose and left to make their way back to the barn at the bottom of the grade—so they could pull up the next stagecoach.

Somewhere around 1907, the first horseless carriage made its appearance on the grade, a forerunner of things to come. A few years later, Miles and Parish began experimenting with motorbuses, but they had a difficult time finding one that could make it up the Tollhouse grade. At one point, three auto firms provided vehicles for demonstration or test runs, but none could make it up the hill with any kind of a load.

"Then we tried a Stanley Steamer and it went up fine until it ran out of water. So we had to stop part of the way up, jack up the wheels, get some

During the late 1920s—after the loss of Ockenden and the Shaver stores—the Bretz general store carried on as the only supply center in the area until 1930.

Beginning around 1911 auto races were run between Tollhouse and Pine Ridge. The competition was as much man-against-mountain as it was machine-against-machine. Known as one of the toughest racecourses in California, the event served as a test of durability among early manufacturers of horseless carriages.

more water and get it started pumping again. Then we made it the rest of the way up,'' Miles said.

Parish apparently was the first person ever to drive a truck up the grade.

In 1914, the two secured a contract to carry mail to the Shaver Lake area. The mails did get through, but it was often difficult work, particularly during inclement weather, when snow, mud or washouts made their appointed rounds anything but easy.

"I had to take some of the mail and crawl across some of the streams on tree limbs, and deliver it to the little communities on foot,'' Parish said. Even the postman was a pioneer in those days.

The partnership broke up a few years later when Parish became ill, but Miles carried on for years and prospered. In 1936 he organized Miles and Sons Trucking Service and went on to become one of the major carriers in the West. His "training'' on the old Tollhouse road had served him well.

About the time that Miles and Parish were turning to Stanley Steamers, a growing number of Fresnans were turning their own Fords, Buicks, Overlands and Studebakers up the mountainside. For those early motorists this was the "Golden Age of Automobiling'' and each trip had to be approached with great caution and care.

During the World War I period, Benson noted, road races were run up the old toll road to the old Armstrong's way station.

In 1919, Isabel Neil Baird, a young Fresnan, made her first motor trip to Shaver Lake, with her mother driving. It was an adventure to remember.

"We loaded the car with about everything we could cram into it, loading up even the sideboards. Since we were going for the summer, we had to take everything we wanted as there were no stores at Shaver Lake at that time.

"Unlike the other women, my mother drove all the way—my father remained in town to tend to the store—forcing that old car up that rough and rutted road.

"It was a daring thing to do in those days,'' she recalled.

Over the years many other cars followed, along with the inevitable flat tires, blown radiators, vapor locks and a host of other automotive problems. In 1922, a "new'' Tollhouse Road was constructed. Although the road remained a twisting, turning approach, it heralded a new era. Faster autos cut the long one-day stagecoach ride from Fresno to Shaver to four or five hours. And a White truck—even with its solid tires and chain drives—could get up the road in one day—instead of three or more. A new age was dawning over the mountains.

CHAPTER SEVEN

Tom Ockenden and Others

One of America's great historians, Frederick Jackson Turner, once observed that the development of Western America seemed to follow a sequence or pattern. First came the explorers, such as John Charles Fremont and, in the case of Yosemite and the central Sierra, Joseph R. Walker. Right behind came the mountain man, still exploring the wilderness but hoping to make his fortune trading or trapping furs. He was followed by the miners, loggers, sheep and cattlemen—pioneers all.

Along the wagon road to Pine Ridge there came other pioneers who would leave their mark upon the unfolding map of Shaver Lake.

The individual who wore the most hats was Thomas J. Ockenden, a native of Southampton, England, and a graduate of Oxford University. Ockenden came to the United States by way of New Zealand in 1886. Shortly after his arrival he made his way to Academy, where he opened a general store. He next moved to Tollhouse and established another store—going into business against Charles Yancey, the hamlet's first merchant and innkeeper. At that time, Tollhouse was a popular overnight stop for those traveling up the mountain. It had a population of 250 persons, a livery, three hotels and an equal number of saloons.

Still, Ockenden kept looking toward the mountains above. Eventually he purchased 2,000 acres near today's Timberwine subdivision.

Ockenden's reputation suggests that he was a classic, that is, a proper Englishman. He was a large, confident, self-made man, whose ambition and dreams loomed as big as the Sierra. How he acquired his wealth remains a mystery. Later in life, Ockenden told Roy Boothe, one of the early forest rangers, that the only way a young man could get ahead was to get in debt as much as possible. Then, if that person had "the right stuff" he would eventually pull out and acquire more property and more wealth. It was, perhaps, the formula Ockenden had used himself.

Ockenden apparently came to the Pine Ridge area a year or so after his older brother, William, had gone into the lumber business with John Humphreys. It was near that site—just below the end of the wagon road where it forked to the Bretz and Musick sawmills—where Tom Ockenden established his Ockenden Ranch.

At that time, the only other business was down the mountainside near the original Humphreys-Mock sawmill. Here, August Beringhoff—Gus Bering —a former mill worker, had set up the first general store on Pine Ridge back in the mid-1870s.

Over the next thirty-plus years Ockenden Hotel and Resort became a favorite stopping spot for those venturing into the Sierra by way of Pine Ridge. From mid-April to early November—as long as the wagon road remained passable—the Ockenden Ranch stood as a welcome stop for those forcing their way up the tortuous wagon road.

Later on, Ockenden entered the cattle business, from which he supplied his slaughterhouse and stores. At one time, Forest Service records indicate, Ockenden held one of the largest grazing permits in the area, running 700 head of cattle out of Statum Meadows.

More than anything, Ockenden was the first to see the recreational and leisure-time possibilities the mountains offered. The mild summers, the sylvan meadows and quiet forests were the only sensible alternatives to the scorching heat of the valley—his British background told him so.

"For many years around the turn of the century—long before there was a Shaver Lake—the Ockenden was it. It was 'the' place," said Alice "Tyke" Carleton, a grandniece of Ockenden.

At its height, his facilities included not only a hotel and general store but cabins, tents on platforms, a dance hall, a butcher shop and a stable.

"The Ockenden became a big attraction for many of the loggers and sawmill workers: it was the only place where a stiff drink could be obtained, since alcoholic beverages were forbidden at the big Shaver mill," said Cliff Field, veteran Pine Ridge resident.

"Tom Ockenden was a sharp businessman. He used to have an inexpensive chicken dinner, and the sawmill workers would come down for dinner and then he would start selling them beer. He even provided burlap bags so they could carry a few bottles back to the bunkhouse."

He also "grubstaked" many of the smaller sawmills in the area, knowing that as the main supply and support center, he would eventually get his money back.

At trail's end in the 1880s, Tom Ockenden's original ranch stood light years removed from today's paved roads and plush condos.

In 1914, Ockenden established a post office at his resort, further solidifying his position as the prime hotel and way station. He also married Mary Emma Summers; his first wife had died some years earlier.

For all his attributes, Ockenden remained somewhat out-of-place in the mountain frontier. It may have been his British accent or mannerisms; others blamed his unusual attire, baggy knickers and necktie.

"He was not the Western stockman-type at all, but rather the indoor businessman, with small or picayunish characteristics in his methods of dealing with other men, and for this reason was disliked by practically all of the stockmen," Boothe related.

Ockenden also had a reputation as a womanizer, who would dispatch his men workers down the mountainside—on spurious errands—so he could make advances to their wives.

Despite these quirks, he was a man of ambition and vision—one who

Tom Ockenden, pioneer Pine Ridge businessman and resort owner.
Dressed in their Sunday best, early Ockenden Ranch campers found a new way of life at the mountain resort. With a general store, hotel, restaurant, livery stable and post office, the ranch catered to all who made their way up Pine Ridge. Circa 1902.

A time of innocence and wonder: For the turn-of-the-century youngsters, few experiences rivaled a summer at the Ockenden Ranch.

could see the potential of the Pine Ridge and Shaver Lake area. When the first tourists began making their way up the mountainside in the 1890s, Ockenden was there to serve them.

Up to that time, the center of commerce had been down the hillside at the community of Pine Ridge. In 1883, before Ockenden's arrival, Adolph Lane and L. B. Frazel had acquired the Bering property and had made several improvements. In 1894, the property changed hands again when Fred Silas

By the turn of the twentieth century, the Ockenden Ranch had emerged as the mountain mecca for many mountain-bound travelers. Valley residents, seeking relief from summer's heat, often stayed for the season. Loggers and teamsters found their way to the ranch for a hot meal or a cold brew.

Kenyon purchased the property. By then, Pine Ridge had a saloon, a livery and a blacksmith shop, besides the general store and a small school. Pine Ridge changed hands again in 1903, when John W. and James Armstrong purchased the site. From that time until the early 1930s it was known as "Armstrongs," or the Pine Ridge Tavern. In April 1921, the Armstrongs sold the resort of approximately 370 acres to Lena Shaver, widow of C. B. Shaver, when it became the Shaver Ranch.

By then other changes had touched the mountains. Some time in the early 1920s, during the winter when the Ockenden was closed for the season, the big hotel was destroyed by fire. It was never rebuilt.

When informed of the fire at his Fresno home, Ockenden's only comment centered around the fact that "a lot of good whiskey had been needlessly destroyed"—or so the story goes.

Ockenden died at Fresno on December 20, 1939. For a few years thereafter, his widow continued to operate the remaining facilities, offering cabins and camping platforms to those who came to enjoy what Tom Ockenden had discovered years earlier.

Today nothing remains of the original Ockenden Ranch, the Pine Ridge Tavern or Widow Waite's. Much like their founders, they made their mark on the emerging map of the mountain area, then faded into Pine Ridge's rich and colorful past.

Turn-of-the-century travelers arrive by stage at the Ockenden Ranch, following a two-day trip from Fresno. For many years, Tom Ockenden's center was the end-of-the-line for those venturing into the Shaver area. The big hotel was destroyed by fire in the 1920s.

In the early 1900s, the hotel and cabins at Armstrong's on Pine Ridge served as a summer haven for many valley residents. Later purchased by Lena Shaver as the Shaver Ranch, the building burned in the 1930s.

CHAPTER EIGHT

Power and Pleasure for the People

Of all the forces that shaped today's Shaver Lake area, none was more important than the genius of John W. Eastwood, the engineer who became the guiding light for hydroelectric development in the San Joaquin River Canyon.

Born in 1857 at his parents' farm in Scott County, Minnesota, Eastwood inherited an interest in engineering and water from his Dutch ancestors. After graduating from State Normal School at Mankato in 1878, Eastwood went to work on the Pacific extension of the Minneapolis and St. Louis Railroad.

Five years later, after hearing of opportunities in the West, Eastwood arrived in Fresno, accompanied by his bride of a few weeks, Ella Tabor. Here in the fledgling community of 10,000 population, he set up a private engineering practice. A year later he made a preliminary survey for a railroad which would bring the lumber down the Tollhouse grade bluff. While the railroad was never built, it provided Eastwood with the opportunity to explore the Sierra and the San Joaquin River basin.

When Fresno was incorporated as a city in 1885, Eastwood was hired to survey routes and construct streets and canals. His competence was soon recognized, and later that year he became the city's first engineer. Eastwood continued his private practice, engineering rail lines, bridges, flumes and other projects for other clients, including, eventually, Shaver's firm.

At that time, the enormous potential for electricity was virtually unknown. Yet Eastwood could see its potential for pumping water for the otherwise arid valley area. Remembering the deep canyons and cascading rivers he had seen en route to the Shaver mill, he began exploring the rugged canyon.

These trips confirmed everything he had seen earlier, and more. After further study, Eastwood contacted several Fresno businessmen and presented a bold development plan. One of those he approached was John

Seymour, the president and largest stockholder of the Fresno Water Company. After considerable effort, they formed the San Joaquin Electric Company, with Seymour as president and Eastwood as vice president and chief engineer.

On April 1, 1895, the company began work on its first powerhouse, located on what was then known as the north fork of the San Joaquin River—today's Willow Creek. Eastwood's plan was to capture the water power where the river began its rapid drop into the main canyon.

Eastwood was on the leading edge of a new age, "powering" new ground. "Everything was experimental," he acknowledged years later.

Construction of San Joaquin No. 1 Powerhouse moved along rapidly, although the project was not without problems. Critics charged that the design and concept were too far-out. In particular, they said the "head," that is, the 1,400 feet the water would drop, was too great. It would create pressures greater than any existing hydro plant of the time, some 600 pounds a square inch! Other skeptics questioned the wisdom of trying to transmit the generated power to Fresno, some thirty-seven miles away. None of the existing power plants in the world had a head that high or a transmission line that long. Eastwood was placing "hope before reason," they charged, by tackling two major problems.

A year later, Eastwood silenced most of those critics when the facility began generating power. Notwithstanding its promising start, the San Joaquin Electric Company soon ran into trouble. Two consecutive drought years started the difficulties. A break in the penstock coupled with a shortage of capital subsequently forced the fledgling company into deeper trouble. But the main trouble came from its main competitor, the Fresno Gas and Electric Company. At that time, there were no utility service districts; competition from the gas-fired, electrical generating firm was fierce. The gas company made an end run on the San Joaquin Electric Company by dispatching workers to the drainage where they filed riparian water claims, effectively shutting off the vital water supply. In some convoluted way, the likes of Miller & Lux had struck again.

Even though the San Joaquin Power Company built a diversion ditch to replace the lost water, the company soon succumbed to a lack of backup generating facilities and capital, declaring bankruptcy in 1899.

Both Seymour and Eastwood lost heavily in the failure.

Although devastated, Eastwood endured. Within a few weeks he was back in the mountains—older and wiser—realizing that any successful hydroelectric system would require vast and sustained amounts of stored water.

For weeks he roamed the wilderness of the upper San Joaquin River, alone and unaided, calculating stream flows and suitable dam sites, guided by a burning desire to succeed.

"I can remember Mr. Eastwood coming up to Shaver with a small burro. He would buy supplies at the small store and then head back into the wilderness alone, recalled Lewella Forkner.

"It was a rather pitiful scene and I felt sorry for him. He had worked for my father redesigning the early flume and dam. He also had been involved in setting out the sawmill's railway to Dinkey Creek, but we had no idea what he was doing on these latter trips."

What emerged out of these travels was typically Eastwood: bigger, better and bolder by a quantum jump. His dream involved a vast hydroelectric system comprised of a series of reservoirs, connected by a network of tunnels, where the water would be used again and again as it dropped down the mountainside.

"This was an exploration saga unique in the annals of early power development. With only a string of horses and pack mules to carry his equipment, the indomitable Eastwood alone explored the rocky gorges and watershed of the region," William A. Myers wrote in his history of the Southern California Edison Company.

Looking about for a developer capable of matching his plans, Eastwood turned to the Pacific Light and Power Company of Los Angeles, which eventually merged with today's Southern California Edison Company.

"It gives me great pleasure to inform you that I have completed the survey for a tunnel line to the junction of Pitman and Big Creek and I can place before you the most remarkable power project yet presented," Eastwood wrote in 1902 to William G. Kerckhoff, a Los Angeles entrepreneur, who would subsequently join with railroad magnate Henry Huntington to develop power in the area.

Kerckhoff also could see the potential. Shortly thereafter Eastwood was placed on the company's payroll and began preparing designs and plans. When Eastwood's report was completed in 1905, Huntington was attracted to the project by its sheer size; evidently it was one that could rival his uncle's, Collis P. Huntington's, efforts to span the West with rails.

Meanwhile, Seymour was reorganizing the San Joaquin Electric Company as the San Joaquin Power Company, which he would subsequently

John S. Eastwood, 1857-1924, civil hydraulic engineer, pioneer in power and logging, ranks as one of Shaver Lake's foremost visionaries.

Facing page: A young John S. Eastwood and two Musick boys pose inside a giant tree on Pine Ridge in 1884. In the following years, the brilliant engineer became Fresno's first city engineer; served the Shaver mill; and planned the Big Creek hydroelectric system.

sell to Kerckhoff and A. C. Balch—after Huntington had acquired control of Pacific Light and Power Company. In turn, Kerckhoff and Balch hired A. G. Wishon as manager. Wishon not only put Eastwood's original plant into good operating condition, but set the groundwork for other units to come. Reorganized in 1905, and incorporated in 1910 as San Joaquin Light and Power Corporation, Eastwood's original powerhouse became part of Pacific Gas and Electric Company in 1930.

By this time Southern California Edison Company was well established in the upper San Joaquin River Canyon, where John Eastwood's dream was a generating reality.

"In its day, Eastwood's Big Creek project was the largest hydroelectric facility ever built. It was rivaled only by the construction of the Panama Canal," observed Roy Walker, a deceased, longtime SCE employee.

With its integrated system of dams, tunnels and powerhouses, the SCE network gave validity to the slogan that the Big Creek waters were the "hardest-working waters in the world."

But Eastwood was not to share either in their reality or their rewards. Apparently Huntingon felt that the project was too big for one man. When work was finally begun in 1910, the engineering firm of Stone and Webster Engineering Corporation was hired to guide the work.

For his labors and water rights, Eastwood was assigned a large block of PL&P stock. But as work proceeded on the costly project, assessments were made against those securities. Eastwood was forced to surrender shares to cover the cost of the assessments. Eventually, he was left with nothing— nothing except the satisfaction that he had engineered the most ambitious hydroelectric project ever conceived by one man.

In 1914, with the Big Creek work well underway, Stone and Webster engineers began looking at the adjoining areas, including the logged-over lands surrounding the Shaver millpond. Eastwood had not included the Stevenson Creek in his original plans; at that time, the sawmill was a going concern—and one of his better clients.

When the sawmill community saw the surveyors running their transits high above the level of the existing millpond, they knew something was afoot. A few months earlier, heavy snows had devastated the aging flume, destroying several sections of the vital water delivery system. Unable to raise funds to rebuild the flume, the Hume-Bennett Lumber Company ceased operations. The sawmill into which Shaver and Swift had poured their energies stood still; for the first time in more than twenty years, the big saws

A Shay locomotive, the workhorse of the logging railroads, heads toward the Shaver millpond with a load of logs. The Shaver Lake Railroad utilized two Shay engines on its logging lines. A smaller Pine Ridge mill also had its own railroad.

were quiet. The workers then began drifting away to other jobs, or to World War I, then emerging in distant lands.

By 1917, with Big Creek power the mainstay of Los Angeles' water supply and with Henry Huntington near retirement, Southern California Edison Company acquired Pacific Light and Power Company. A year later, engineers began finalizing Eastwood's original plan by starting construction of Florence Lake and the Ward tunnel.

Then in 1919, SCE began the purchase of most of the Hume-Bennett Shaver properties for $1.4 million, ultimately acquiring some 32,000 acres. The purchase of the sawmill proved to be a prudent move. Within two years, as SCE's Shaver Lake Lumber Company, the mill was cutting once more; but this time, the lumber was going up the mountainside—to be used in the construction of other dams and powerhouses.

In preparation for a new Shaver dam, a spur line from the San Joaquin and Eastern Railroad's Dawn station was constructed in 1925. Work on the dam itself began a year later.

Robert Bretz of Clovis was a young boy at the time, but he vividly recalls the activity. His father and 125 other workers were involved in clearing vegetation from the basin.

"My dad moved in a portable steam mill and hired a large crew of workers. They spent the better part of two years cutting and stacking the material, using what lumber they could but burning all the small material. It was a big job," Bretz recalled.

Over at the dam site, hundreds of workers were involved in setting forms and pouring concrete—except during the winter when freezing weather prohibited such activities. At the same time hard-rock miners were busy, pushing two underground tunnels. One would deliver water from Huntington Lake. A discharge tunnel would take Shaver water to Powerhouse 2A in the Big Creek canyon.

The dam was the third and largest within the Big Creek system. It stood 170 feet above the streambed and its crest stretched out 2,169 feet. The big barrier impounded 135,000 acre feet of water—nearly the combined capacities of Huntington and Florence lakes—twenty-seven times larger than the old millpond.d

The Shaver Lake dam was finished October 23, 1927. A month later, workers and a handful of spectators gathered one evening as the old mill buildings were put to the torch—a strange and ignominious conclusion to the dreams of C. B. Shaver and Harvey Swift, now dead more than twenty years. A few months later, the first unit of the new powerhouse annex began spinning, using water impounded at Shaver Lake.

It was another year before the dam would fill; several years would elapse before the recreational potential of the new reservoir would be realized. But a new "Shaver Lake" was on the scene, ready to provide power and pleasure to a growing number of Californians.

CHAPTER NINE

"R&R" Come to Shaver Lake

If logging was the foundation for the development of the original sawmill community of Shaver, then rest and recreation became the force in shaping Shaver Lake's reputation as Fresno's favorite watering hole.

The genesis of the Shaver area as a rest spot reaches back to the days of Mono Indian migrations. Even the first white explorers could see the land was a gentle wilderness, whose sparkling streams and lush meadows marked an inviting stopping point. Indeed, the Stevenson Creek basin was a special land. While the creek and most of the high Sierra streams were barren of fish prior to the arrival of the white man, carp were introduced shortly after the millpond had been filled—as an accommodation to the large number of German and Scandinavian millworkers from Michigan. Trout came next, made as "coffee can" transplants from nearby drainages. A decade later, perch and bass were planted.

Keeping a good fishing hole a secret was as hard in the early 1900s as it is today. As more and bigger fish were caught, a growing number of Fresnans began testing the waters of the millpond—usually with good results. In 1902, M. W. Muller and J. Ed Hughes, two Fresno businessmen, officers in the state militia, and—more importantly—fishing enthusiasts, spent a couple of weeks at the millpond with a half dozen other devoted anglers. The outing was a smashing success. "Let's do it again next year," suggested one of the group.

The following summer, two dozen friends were invited along, and they, too, were hooked on the millpond as a fishing hole. Somewhere along the line, someone cast out the suggestion that the hail-and-hearty, well-met group should organize, and thus the legendary Shaver Lake Fishing Club was born, with twenty-two charter members and Muller as president.

The next summer at Shaver was even more stimulating. Since there were no overnight accommodations, Muller commandeered some of the militia's tents and set up a rather impressive fishing camp. The enthusiastic members

Founded around 1900, the Sulphur Meadow campground served the Shaver millpond's first campers. Located about a half-mile from the sawmill, the camp was popular with friends and families of the millworkers. By 1911, the camp had a small golf course—and even electricity from the mill.

came up on horseback—a long, two-day ride. Professional chefs were brought in and prepared big spreads. Tuxedos became the uniform-of-the-day. Officials of the lumber company were invited to dinner, led by no other than C. B. Shaver and Harvey Swift, who were soon caught up in the camaraderie of the club.

By the next summer, Shaver had arranged for the construction of a small clubhouse, set on the eastern shore of the millpond, which spurred additional interest in the club. In the ensuing years, the fishing club grew in size and stature—further strengthening the ties between Fresno and the sawmill community.

"In a group of amateur fishermen such as members of the Shaver Lake Fishing Club, it was to be expected that many tall fishing stories would emerge. As summer after summer passed, the fish stories got wilder and wilder. A few of the members developed real talent for fiction in this department. Competition in landing record-sized fish became so keen that one of the members who had read of Mark Twain's jumping frog, resorted to buckshot to make his trout weigh more than that of his nearest competitor," Edwin Eaton wrote in his book, *Vintage Fresno.*

"Shaver Lake Fishers Gather," proclaimed the *Fresno Bee and Republican* of April 17, 1927. "Fresno Prevaricators Spin Fishin' Yarns."

M. W. Muller, first president, and Ed Hughes, joint founders of the Shaver Lake Fishing Club.
Members of the Shaver Lake Fishing Club gather during an early 1900s outing. Third-generation descendants of those original anglers continue to whip the waters of Shaver Lake today.

Members of the Shaver Lake Fishing Club gather at their clubhouse in 1924. Down the years, the members have been more durable than their buildings. Club co-founder Ed Hughes stands second from right, back row.

Facing page: Shaver Lake Fishing Club members test their luck on the waters of the millpond in the early 1900s.

The Shaver Lake Fishing Club's first clubhouse. The vintage organization has had more luck fishing than in keeping its clubhouses. Three buildings have fallen victim to either snow, storms or fire.

"The best liars of Fresno County swapped big ones last night, and—nobody won.

"The tales they told were 'high, wide and handsome,' but they were so tall that not even their intimates took hook, line or sinker," the story continued.

A month later, the newspaper announced the twenty-third annual summer meeting—for the more serious matter of removing the clubhouse in preparation for the completion of the new dam.

The founding members of the Shaver Lake Fishing Club made their last cast years ago. Today, the thinning ranks of the second generation members reminisce about the good old days—along with the big ones that got away. Meanwhile the third generation carries on a tradition that gets larger with each cast.

"It was quite an elite group: judges, doctors and the town leaders. We had a fishing derby and a lot of fun. Those were wonderful, wonderful times," reflected Willis Good, a second generation member of the club.

The club did have a difficult time with its clubhouse, however. Heavy snows collapsed the first structure in 1907. The creation of the new lake in 1927 took the site of the second. Deep snows and a Mono wind destroyed the third structure in 1948. Through it all, the Shaver Lake Fishing Club has endured.

Despite its fishing fame, it was winter sports that gave Shaver Lake its identification as a year-round recreation area. The first step of that development came in the winter of 1905, when the Shaver family, accompanied by several other friends, made a rare winter visit to the snowbound sawmill. Using a horse-drawn wagon with sleds—one kept at the mill for the winter crew—C. B. Shaver arranged for the wagon to go down to snowline to pick up the group and carry them to the Shaver cabin.

For several days the group delighted in the sunny snowscape. Snow play—building snowmen and snowball fights—led the winter fun. A few daring members of the group tried sliding around on wood slats attached to their boots—crude skis, similar to those the iron miners and loggers had used back in Michigan. The activities were great fun and consumed much of the daylight hours. Feasting, storytelling and huddling around the small wood stove occupied the winter evenings. It was a special time, and those involved reveled in the clear, crisp winter days, which they found much more pleasant than the dreary fog and cold in the valley.

Two years later C. B. Shaver was dead. Another decade would pass before the Commercial Club of Fresno would brave the wintry whiteness of the

Ethel Shaver slides over the snow, using improvised skis at the family cabin at Shaver during a rare winter visit. On occasion, during the early 1900s, the Shaver family and friends enjoyed the winter wonders at the snowbound mill—long before most Californians were thinking of winter sports.

Sierra, holding the First Annual Ice and Snow Carnival at Huntington Lake in 1916.

It would be years before winter recreation would appear in earnest. But the ice had been broken—so had the perception that the Sierra winter was a harsh, hostile, impenetrable white prison.

In between, the thrust of Sierra recreation remained focused on the summer months. Not surprisingly, a growing number of summer campers and fishermen discovered what an aging Tom Ockenden had been promoting for the past twenty-five years: Summer and the Sierra go together.

By the summer of 1914—nearly fifteen years before the enlarged Shaver Lake came on the scene—the Sulphur Meadows area, located on the eastern

shore about half a mile south of the big sawmill, had already become a
popular camping area, with electric lights and a nine-hole golf course. The
millpond had its fish. Nearby, the streams and woodlands welcomed those
interested in hiking, picnicking or nature study.

Once the valley schools adjourned for vacation, families began heading
for Sulphur Meadows campground, seeking relief from the heat of the valley
or joining their fathers on their day off from the mill or Big Creek project.

"The campground is filled to capacity already," the U.S. Forest Service's
district ranger reported as early as July 1, 1914.

But the Big Creek project was to touch Shaver in other ways. Four months
later, Frank Price, district ranger, made his monthly report:

> It is rumored that the Pacific Light and Power Corporation is contem-
> plating raising Shaver Lake by putting a dam a short distance below the
> old dam, with the idea of getting power for two more powerhouses on
> Stevenson Creek. A survey party has been engaged running a flood line
> 100 feet above the present lake level. If this is accomplished, the village of
> Shaver Lake, including the mill and the Shaver Ranger Station, will be
> submerged.

When the news eventually filtered down it came as a thunderbolt to the
small sawmill community. Shaver's widow, Lena, followed the announce-
ment with great concern. Recognizing that a larger dam would cover the
small cabin she had come to revere, she acted swiftly. Gathering a few close
friends, she proposed that they look for a new site. The spot she had in mind
was located about a mile to the southwest, on the rocky eastern slope of
Stevenson Mountain. Once there was some agreement to the location, she
had her son-in-law, Dr. Harry Craycroft, purchase 160 acres on the lower
slopes of the mountainside. Once title was cleared, Mrs. Shaver had her
home cabin torn apart, piece by piece, and relocated to the new site, known
as Rock Haven.

Organized in 1921 as a corporation, Rock Haven had sixteen partners,
drawn from some of Fresno's finest families—half of whom were affiliated
with the medical community in the valley.

In that first year, according to Isabell Neil Baird, Drs. and Mesdames O. B.
Doyle, J. C. Cooper, and Dwight Trowbridge, Sr. along with W. O. Miles,
Luther P. Neil and William Sutherland built their homes. Summer homes,
as such, were on their way to Shaver.

"We had a late spring that first year and it was very hard to get the

By the spring of 1926, workers were busy clearing the site of the Shaver Lake dam. The old sawmill and millpond—their days numbered—are visible left.

building started," Mrs. Baird recalled. "Bill Maupin and Lloyd Baird, along with a couple of friends from the university, cleared the land with the help of two gray mules, hauling rocks and logs away.

"All the lumber for the homes had to be hauled up from the valley on trucks with hard rubber wheels; finished lumber was not available at the local mills," she added.

Without such constraints as building permits or inspectors, the houses went up rapidly, with the workers living nearby in tents, set up to expedite construction.

In the following years, other Rock Haven members built their cabins, setting the framework for a whole new dimension to summer living for Shaver Lake.

"Before there was such a thing as air conditioning, anyone who could would try to get to the mountains for the summers," said Mrs. Baird. "As soon as school was out, they would pack up and head for Shaver or Huntington lakes and stay all summer. The husbands would remain in town and tend the shops and offices, then come up on weekends.

By September 1927, the "new" Shaver Lake dam was close to completion, rising above the old millponds that rest in the background, left. Looking south, Shaver Point stands at the far right.

67 9-1-27

703

On an autumn evening in 1927—in a climactic moment—the sawmill and logging community of Shaver were deliberately burned to make way for a new and enlarged Shaver Lake. The remains of the old dam, center, still lie at the bottom of the existing lake bed—some 120 feet beneath the high water line.

"It was the hot summers in Fresno and the valley that made Shaver and Rock Haven such a popular place."

When the menfolk did arrive, they brought additionàl supplies of fresh foods—and their fishing poles.

Other forces continued to push the recreational bandwagon. In 1930, a year after the enlarged Shaver Lake was filled, Fresno County supervisors, hard pressed by Great Depression austerity—but pushed even harder by constiutents who could only mourn the submerged Sulphur Meadows site—established a new campground on Shaver Point.

If the old millpond was a great fishing hole, the new and enlarged Shaver Lake was even better. The new campground caught on quickly. Up until the advent of the year-round trout season, the opening of the fishing season was the highlight of the Shaver Lake year, with anglers strung out all around its twenty-two-mile shoreline.

"We always had one hell of a crowd for that opening day," commented John Harshman, who came to Shaver Lake in 1928 and founded the Trading Post, Shaver Lake's first business. "I think every fisherman in the valley must have been up here; sometimes we would have 3,000 fishermen strung out along the shoreline. It was some sight."

Harshman also became Shaver Lake's first postmaster. In 1932, he married Velma Dalton, and together they raised a family on the second floor of their small store, eventually establishing Johnny's on Shaver Point and subdividing other sections in the area.

"When I went there, the new dam had just been completed and there were few workers around. There were only two little cabins in Shaver Heights and the sixteen cabins at Rock Haven.

"It was rough getting a business going. Those were rough times—even for eating," Harshman recalled.

In 1935, Charlie Eckert married Elsie Peterson, the daughter of timber operator Herman Peterson, and together they built Eckert's Resort up the road from the Trading Post. They opened the Fourth of July 1936, but the resort operated only a few weeks before it was destroyed by fire. Undaunted, the Eckerts rebuilt and hung on through the Great Depression, serving those early visitors and vacationers.

They also served meals to the Depression-born Work Projects Administration crews. One of the Eckerts' boarders was John Hodgkins, a young Fresnan who had discovered the thrills and spills of skiing with the Fresno Ski Club at Park Ridge and Badger Pass.

The Pitman-Huntington Tunnel pours its filling waters into Shaver Lake by way of Tunnel Creek.

For Shaver Lake fans and the Southern California Edison Company, few things are sweeter than a full lake.

The Shaver dam, 170 feet high and 2,169 feet long, creates a lake twenty-seven times larger than the original millpond.

Campers crowd the shore of Shaver Lake in 1955, near the Dorabelle Campground. Ever since the millpond was set in place in the 1890s, fishermen and campers have flocked to the mountain area, helping to sustain Shaver's identity.

Facing page: Before the advent of the year-round trout fishing season, opening day brought the biggest crowds of the year to Shaver Lake. Thousands of anglers flocked to the lake to test their sills. In 1955, when Shaver Lake had but a dozen year-round residents, it counted more than 3,000 opening-day fishermen.

For most of the 1930s, Shaver Lake was little more than a summer fishing hole, waiting to be discovered by Californians yet unborn. The Shaver Point "fishing fleet" bears little resemblance to the present marina.

Winter sports buffs line road at Shaver Point during the late 1930s, when John Hodgkins operated a small ski tow on the north slope. Inconsistent snows forced the closure of the ski area after a few unsuccessful winters.

While working with a WPA crew clearing brush, he saw the steep north side of Shaver Point and figured it might make a nice little ski area—if it had a rope tow similar to those crude devices showing up on the slopes of New England.

"I found an old car engine and got it running. Then I bought the rope and pulleys, and salvaged some tire rims and got the tow going. I talked the guy who was running the bulldozer for the brush crew into clearing the hill. All together, I didn't have more than a hundred bucks in the whole thing.

"The county was plowing the road at that time and a few skiers were catching onto the sport, so I thought it might be a good idea. I ran it for a couple of winters, charging ten cents a ride or one dollar all day. But I couldn't make any money; the snow wasn't dependable enough, and I finally had to shut it down," Hodgkins related years later.

Nevertheless skiing and winter fun were on the way. In 1957, Knute Flint, who had made some big bucks flying helicopters in South America, established China Peak near Huntington Lake. By this time, the road had become all-weather state Highway 168. In between, the Forest Service had built the Dorabelle Campground; the Fresno Sequoia Council Boy Scouts of America had built Camp Chawanakee, and in the early 1960s, Southern California Edison developed Camp Edison—with each one adding to the appeal of Shaver Lake.

CHAPTER TEN

Law and Order—Shaver Style

Law and order had a tough time making their way up to the mountain area known as Pine Ridge, the pioneers noted.

Though Fresno County was established in 1856, the wilderness around what was to become Shaver Lake did not surrender to the first wave of humanity without tears, toil and strife.

Marauding Indians, claim jumpers, highwaymen, along with range wars between sheep and cattle men, prompted the first calls for government. Accidents and other tragedies intensified the demand for collective action.

Historian Ernestine Winchell recalled the terror that bears or mountain lions struck in the hearts of the early settlers on Pine Ridge. The subsequent destruction of vast timber stands prompted the need for yet other rules and regulations. Forest fires and the need for roads fueled still more calls for government.

To a large extent, the first settlers on Pine Ridge made their own laws—as had others throughout the West. When a prospector saw a potential mining site, he simply claimed it. And when the settler needed a cabin site, he took it under the "right of pre-emption," that is, he "squatted" on the land.

In 1862, Congress, trying to promote Western migration—and generate treasury revenues—passed the Homestead Act, providing up to 160 acres of free or inexpensive land, subject only to the stipulation that the settler live on the land for five years and improve it. The residence requirement could even be deferred by purchasing the property for $1.25 an acre—light years away from the price of Shaver Lake property today.

Whether William Stephenson, the first cattleman on Pine Ridge, homesteaded or squatted in the mountain meadow that was to bear his misspelled name is unclear.

Those arriving a few years later often used the Swamp and Overflow Act, one of the most commonly abused laws of the time. By placing a rowboat on a wagon, and then having a team of horses pull the rowboat across a mountain meadow, a claimant could swear that he had traversed the entrie area in a rowboat—thereby claiming title to what was supposed to be swamplands. Similarly, the Mining Act of 1872, along with the Timber and Stone Act of 1876, provided still other means whereby large parcels of public lands passed into private ownership, leading to the mosaic of public and private lands that surrounds Shaver Lake today.

The pioneer days saw many other abuses of government lands; to some extent, all of the land acts were circumvented regularly. The sawmills, to obtain the volume of timber needed, often hired "entrymen," who—for a price—would file individual claims on timber stands. Once the claimant had title, he would turn the trees over to the mills, which, in many instances, had no other alternative to obtain an adequate supply of sawlogs.

Against this background, it soon became obvious that something needed to be done. The first step came in 1878, when Congress gave the General Land Office of the Department of Interior the responsibility of managing millions of acres of public lands. By 1880, the era of "free cutting" was over, marked by the arrival of government survey crews who began the massive task of mapping the mountainous area of eastern Fresno County.

Besides setting the corners, the surveyors had to verify lands that had passed into private ownership. In many cases the surveys were poorly done or not done at all, setting the stage for boundary-line disputes that continue today. When the surveys were done, responsibility was turned over to the federal land commissioner at Stockton.

By the end of 1881, advertisements for timber sales began appearing in the *Mariposa Gazette*, subject to any prior or possibly unverified claims. Even when timber contracts were sold, the inadequate enforcement did little to stem the abuses that went with "cut-and-run" logging.

For many newcomers, the trees on Pine Ridge stood as an inexhaustible supply—just waiting to be utilized. Others felt the vast stands were obstacles to progress and safety and needed to be cut down so the wilderness could be tamed.

But there were a few warning voices in the Western wilderness, decrying the over-grazing on public lands and the destruction of forest lands. Already John Muir's sermons on the mountains were being heard. Other conservationists were predicting a "timber famine," or even worse, the ruination of the public lands.

In 1891, at the urging of the California Legislature, Congress authorized the creation of a forest reserve system, providing the first measure of protection for the forest lands. Two years later, on February 14, 1893, the Sierra

The pioneer families came from hardy stock—to be tested and tempered by the tall trees and big mountains on Pine Ridge. Despite often primitive living conditions—and an absence of government—their descendants—Humphreys, Bretz, Peterson, Yancey and Musick—have not only survived, but thrived along the way.

Forest Reserve was created by President Benjamin Harrison. It stood as the tenth designated reserve, the largest in the nation—nearly four times larger than any of its predecessors. It would be managed by the General Land Office, under the Department of the Interior.

A headquarters was eventually established at North Fork. About 1898, sixty rangers were hired to patrol the vast reserve that embraced much of today's Yosemite high country, lands now in the Inyo, Stanislaus and Sequoia national forests, as well as today's Kings Canyon National Park. While those selected were unfamiliar with such sciences as forestry and range management, the officers were generally faithful, honest and hard-working individuals who had more land and problems than they could possibly manage.

For these early rangers, the protection of timber stands and the removal of trespassing sheep comprised their principal duties. Gene Tully, one of the original Sierra rangers, blazed trails, marked timber for sale, issued grazing permits and tried to address Indian land claims. He is credited with removing trespassing sheepmen from many sections of the Sierra.

In most cases men like Tully worked alone, patrolling vast areas of the mountains.

"It was a hard, lonely and sometimes dangerous life. Sudden illness, a fall, weather, slides and the threatened vengeance of a resentful stockman made early rangers always watchful," he noted.

Richard L. P. Bigelow, another early ranger, once had to shoot and wound a sheepman to get the herder's attention.

"We rangers had to pack guns to protect ourselves. We did not like the orders to withdraw and there were no withdrawals that I ever heard of," he reported.

Government of a more enlightened sort came to the area in 1895, when a school district was formed at Shaver, centered around a one-room school-house. This lone bastion of education had been built by Lewis P. Swift at the insistence of the wives of the permanent mill employees, who felt it was imperative that the children have a formal education.

"It was a very small school, and we had trouble keeping it open because the school year didn't coincide with the sawmill season. As I recall there was only a dozen students, with about eight grades of grammar school," Rose Emma Fortner reminisced years later.

"There was a pot-bellied wood stove for heat, and a pail of water from the spring for drinking with a long-handled ladle.

"I didn't go to school there, but my older sister did. However, I did go to the school several times; I would squat on a little rise outside of the window until the children started to giggle and the teacher would ask my sister to take me home.

"This schoolhouse also served as the church . . . and as a mortuary when there was a death in the community."

But it was a lonely outpost in its day, a solitary symbol of hope and enlightenment.

When the wagon carrying the mill's payroll was held up and robbed near Widow Waite's—the first of two such incidents—a futile cry went out, Mrs. Fortner recalled, because it was days after when the sheriff finally arrived on the scene.

For many of those early years, law and order had been a private affair. When Theodore Payne was shot and killed near the Humphreys and Mock sawmill in 1870, it was the neighboring settlers who captured the assailants and took them to Millerton for trial. Other confrontations or crimes were settled on a more expedient basis. It wasn't always justice, but it was usually swift, the old-timers noted.

In 1905, the Sierra Forest Reserve became a national forest under the U.S. Forest Service. Three years later, large blocks were split off to form the

The 1891-1926 Shaver millpond—small by comparison to today's Shaver Lake—served both the sawmill and the flume. Efforts to deliver irrigation water were thwarted by lawsuits over water rights.

Sequoia, Stanislaus, Mono and Inyo national forests. The division still left the Sierra with 1,935,680 acres, the heart of which centered around the aging Shaver millpond.

By this time, Fresno County was on the move, gradually pushing its road system into the mountains. Cattlemen who had wrestled control of the mountain meadows from sheepmen established their homes and corrals at Auberry, Academy and other foothill locations, bringing with them the need for still more government. In 1892, the county purchased the toll road through Auberry and Meadow Lakes, the Fresno and Pine Ridge Toll Road, which had been built four years earlier.

Forest rangers who had been making their rounds on horses soon began pushing their "tin lizzies" up and down either muddy or dusty roadways. Getting around the district proved to be a problem, whether it was by horse or horseless carriage, one Shaver ranger wrote in an early report.

> It is rumored that the government is negotiating for a gasoline car to replace the one in use. The new car will be better constructed to climb grades. Let us hope that it will be well enough constructed to travel by its own power—not ours!

Log chutes and steam-powered cableways served the Fresno Flume and Lumber Company's more remote timberlands. Logging practices were non-existent by today's standards, as evident at right.

By 1909, the old "corduroy log road," which had jolted those traveling around the Shaver millpond, was gone. A slightly improved road had been extended beyond Shaver to Cascada, and then on to Manzanita Park, now known as Big Creek. Spur roads also opened up.

When World War I broke upon the nation, the government turned to the national forests to provide additional forage and lumber for the war effort. A summer office was established at Musick Meadows, where livestock was counted en route to the summer ranges. A hand-crank telephone provided a degree of modern communications, further aiding the cause of government.

Uniforms, long a hit-and-miss affair, became available for rangers. Improving forestry sciences brought new responsibilities. Recreation, hydrology and engineering required a new breed of professionals and the ranks of the Forest Service opened up to accommodate them.

Law and order took a giant step forward in the eastern part of the county in about 1912, with the start-up of the Big Creek project. The arrival of hundreds of workers for the hydroelectric project and the accompanying

Forest fires, such as the disastrous 1931 Tollhouse fire, were an annual terror for the early residents and timber operators around Shaver Lake—even though the sawmill operators were responsible for many of the early conflagrations on Pine Ridge.

San Joaquin and Eastern Railroad, forced the county to place a constable at Auberry.

Athough the SJ&E expedited the delivery of men and materials to the Big Creek construction scene, the loss of the Shaver flume brought great changes to the lumbering scene during World War I and for the next few years after.

The Tollhouse Road, which had been a beast killer for the mule skinners and teamsters, was no less a terror for the early truckers hauling lumber down the mountainside from the Prescott, Peterson and Rout mills.

In the early 1920s, under mounting pressure from timber operators and mountain residents, the county appropriated $90,000 for a new Tollhouse Road. This motor road reduced the grade from 23 to 8 percent; however, it lengthened the trip by more than two miles. It would also make the road safer and more attractive to a growing number of motorists, the *Fresno Republican* reported.

Today, this 1922 road is commonly called the old Tollhouse Road, while the "original" toll road recedes into the mountainside.

In 1933, the road from Fresno to Shaver was incorporated into the emerging state highway system, and its designation changed from Highway 76 to Route 168.

While a handful of Big Creek residents had been pressing for some kind of

Filled for the first time in 1929, Shaver Lake would emerge as a major recreation center in eastern Fresno County—as well as the largest reservoir in Southern California Edison Company's Big Creek system. An improved boat launching ramp was thirty-five years away, however.

Facing page: Early teamster-turned-stage-bus operator W. R. "Billy" Miles, with family, also pioneered snow removal in the early 1930s.

Early efforts at snow removal often fell short of expectations, as all kinds of plows and tractors were pushed into the fray.

Big storms and deep snows often closed the Shaver road for weeks at a time. Acceptable snow removal didn't arrive until the state plows came onto the scene in the 1950s.

snow removal as early as the 1920s, the first attempts at plowing didn't come until the 1930s. At that time, the only year-round residents of Shaver Lake were the founders of the Trading Post resort, John and Velma Harshman, along with Ed Steen, who manned the Forest Service guard station at Musick Creek, and his wife, Doris.

"Billy Miles tried to plow the road, but it was a hit and miss affair—with an emphasis on the 'miss.'" The type of snow removal equipment needed to do the job just didn't exist at that time," Steen observed.

"We used to be snowbound for weeks at a time, and about our only other contacts were the Harshmans, who were just up the road."

Velma Harshman recalled making infrequent trips to Fresno for supplies

Doris and Ed Steen, U.S. Forest Service fire guard, at the Musick Meadow guard station during the 1930s.

Facing page: Winter's snow often closed the road in front of the Trading Post for weeks on end.
Shaver Lake's appeal is a long-standing affair for many. In the 1930s, the W. R. Miles Stage Lines carried youth groups and school classes to Shaver Lake for a day in the snow. An unidentified group poses in front of the Shaver Lake Trading Post. Until skiing took hold at China Peak, winter was a dormant time at Johnny's, Shaver Point.

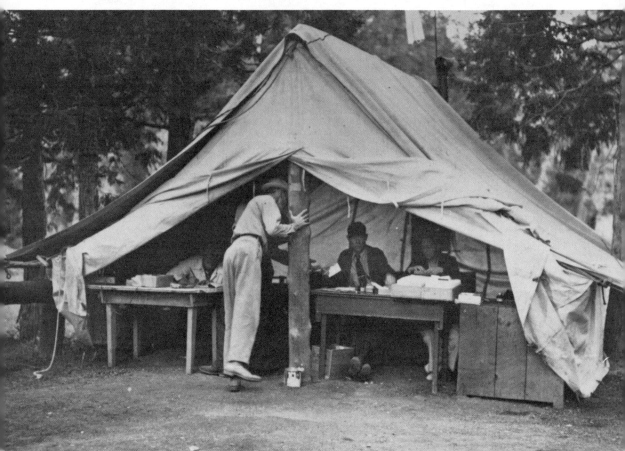

The U.S. Army guarded Shaver Lake dam from possible sabotage during World War II, protecting electrical power for vital defense industries in Southern California.

During the deer hunting seasons of the 1930s, the U.S. Forest Service's guard station was expanded to validate deer tags. Forest guard Ed Steen and his wife, Doris, along with game wardens, staffed the tent facility.

Larry Shannon, perennial fire chief, has taken a lot of heat during the years he has seen Shaver Lake grow from 18 to 1,800 year-round residents.

during those long winters, often having to walk down to the snowline to catch the Miles' stage.

"Even then we never knew if we were going to get back. The roads were so muddy and slippery that it seemed like we would never get back home," she said.

Law and order had other difficulties during the 1930s, according to Hubert "Hube" Nevins, who went to work for the Fresno Sheriff's Office in 1933. During the next twenty years he became a first-line fixture whenever anyone was in trouble in the mountains.

"Before there were radio communications we responded by telephone calls. One night I remember getting a call from one of the bars at Dinkey Creek, with a woman complaining about a fight going on between two patrons.

"I told her there wasn't much I could do about it because it was a three-hour drive from where I was at that point. By the time I could get there the fight would be over; or if it was still going on, the guys involved would be too tough for me to handle," Nevins reminisced.

There were many other incidents of lost or injured hikers or fishermen, and it was Nevins who was usually summoned.

"If I needed help I would drive through Shaver looking for any able man and deputize him on the spot. That's how we got things done in my day."

On some of the early forest fires, such as the Mount Stevenson and Toll-house fires, the Forest Service resorted to similar methods to get firefighters. For other emergencies, the local state game warden or Forest Service's fire guard became the symbol of law and order.

Progress toward road construction and snow removal was slow during World War II. In 1955, the state completed construction of the all-weather highway above Shaver Lake to Huntington Lake, known variously as the Big Creek bypass, the Tamarack Ridge route or Forest Highway 48. Ever since the early 1940s, the state chamber of commerce and the Fresno Ski Club had been promoting a central Sierra ski site. In 1957 China Peak came along, and gave Shaver Lake another push into prominence.

The transportation scene moved forward again in the early 1960s, with the start-up of construction of an eight-mile section of four-lane roadway that would bypass Tollhouse—a route that closely paralleled the old flume.

Today, thousands of motorists zoom up and down Highway 168 with little appreciation of the pioneering that has gone on before them.

Shaver Lake took its first step toward self government in 1957, when it organized its own fire department. Boyd Turner, a local resident and hill manager at China Peak, was named the community's first fire chief. Less than a year later, he resigned and was replaced by Larry Shannon, a retired airline mechanic and hardware store operator, who was still putting out fires thirty years later.

Shaver will mark its first hundred years in 1992—its centennial anniversary. By that time, Shannon believes that Shaver Lake could have its own city government, with perhaps a year-round population of 5,000 and a weekend or holiday population five times that number. Whatever the figure, it will be a long way from the handful of pioneers who endured that first winter in the wilderness a century earlier.

An Untitled Ode

By Gertrude Swift Eaton, Circa 1920

I met my little-girl self
　Up at Shaver just today;
She was standing in our garden
　And she called me in to play.

A happy little youngster,
　Going there in '93,
She had just come back to Shaver
　To spend the years with me.

To live again our childhood,
　The kind of years that last;
So over that changed hillside
　She led me through the past.

We spent an hour in memory
　So she took me by the hand,
And she showed me memory places
　Only I could understand.

We visited the playhouse
　We had built upon the rocks.
And I helped her get the pitch out
　That was tangled in her locks.

We went down to the meadow
　Where we hunted polliwogs,
Then we walked along the skidway
　And watched them hauling logs.

We watched men raising sinkers*
　As we walked along the boom;
We climbed upon the lumber piles
　And walked along the flume.

We listened to the buzzing
　And the humming of the mill,
And we marvelled at the miles of pipe
　That heated up the kiln.

We rode around the tramway
　On the car for miles and miles.
Midst the clapping of the lumber
　As they dropped it on the piles.

We smelled the scent of sawdust
　As it flew from screaming saws;
We watched the lumber rolling
　Toward the edger's wicked claws.

We watched the spillway water
　As we stood upon the dam,
Then we ran up to the cookhouse
　And begged some pie from Sam.

Then to the little schoolhouse
　With Jerry, Joe and Meg.
And we sat upon the big flat stump
　And played at mumble peg.

Then we hunted for white violets
　And picked a lovely bunch
And gave them to the teacher
　While she finished eating lunch.

Then back home to our cabin
　Where we both sat down to rest—
Our little mountain cabin
　Where life was at its best.

*logs too heavy to float

Filled with homemade comforts
  Just as crude as they could be,
But an atmosphere about it
  That is very dear to me.

And while we sat there dreaming
  Of the days of long ago,
My husband beckoned to me
  It was time for us to go.

The golden sun was sinking
  Behind the western hill,
The workmen's tools were put away,
  The ruined mill was still.

We knew that Shaver days had gone,
  The time had come to part;
My little-girl self felt the pang
That struggled in my heart.

She threw her arms around me
  With a frantic cry,
For she felt the separation
  That would come with this goodbye.

So I held her to me closely
  With a sad and throbbing ache,
As I laid her back to slumber
  In the cradle of the lake.

And while I'm looking backward
  To the days where memory clings,
I have a little lad at home**
  Who dreams of bigger things.

He plays he's building bridges
  That might chasms span,
And he says he'll be a builder
  When he grows to be a man.

Who knows but what my little self
  May take him by the hand
And lead this little lad of mine
  On through this Progress Land.

**Lewis S. Eaton of Fresno

Shaver Lake Chronology

5000 B.C. Paiutes Indians from eastern Sierra cross the crest; some eventually remain, marking the arrival of the Western Monos or Monachees. East-west summer trade ensues.

1806 Early Spanish explorers discover and name Kings and San Joaquin rivers; visit North Fork Monos.

1833 Joseph R. Walker crosses central Sierra, sights Yosemite Valley and giant Sequoia.

1844 Capt. John C. Fremont visits foothills between Kings and San Joaquin rivers.

1849 California Gold Rush; white invasion of the Sierra, including southern Sierra.

1851 Camp Barbour (later Fort Miller, Millerton) established to protect settlers and miners from displaced Indians.

1854 James Hultz established first sawmill at Corlew Meadows (Meadow Lakes) on Pine Ridge.

1856 Fresno County formed out of Mariposa County.

1864 California State Survey under Josiah Whitney begins Sierra surveys; names Sarver's Peak for early Tollhouse settler.

1866 Woods brothers begin construction of Tollhouse Road.

1867 Humphreys-Mock mill established near today's Shaver Ranch, the first of nearly fifty sawmills to follow.

1868 First white child born on Pine Ridge.

1875 Joseph Bretz's mill begins cutting—the first of three generations that will continue to harvest trees until mid-1950s.

1878 Fresno County acquires original Tollhouse Road for $5,000.

1880 U.S. Lands Office assumes control for federal lands, ending free cutting on public lands.

1887 Tom Ockenden acquires large holdings on Pine Ridge. A brother, William, buys Donehooe sawmill, which is moved to Ockenden.

1889 Pine Ridge Flume and Irrigation Company begins construction of ill-fated box-shaped flume from Stevenson Creek to Tollhouse.

1891 Fresno Flume and Irrigation Company organized by C. B. Shaver, Lewis P. Swift; acquires rights of Pine Ridge Flume and Irrigation Company and several small sawmills.

1892 Construction starts on Shaver sawmill and camp—marking a major turning point for the mountain meadow.

1893 Storm destroys earthen dam; replacement rock dam started. Work begins on a forty-two-mile-long V-shaped flume to Clovis mill. Sierra Forest Reserve created by President Harrison, with over 4 million acres under Department of Interior.

1890s Hikers and others seeking recreation, following the tracks of the lumber wagons, start treks to Shaver, Dinkey Creek and surrounding Sierra areas.

1898 First forest rangers hired to patrol Sierra Forest Reserve.

1901 Lewis P. Swift, the "man" behind the Shaver mill, dies at Fresno; his brother, Harvey, assumes control of mill.

1902 Shaver Lake Rail Road established; line eventually extended twelve miles toward Dinkey Creek. Shaver Lake Fishing Club organized, producing fish stories of unheralded proportions.

1903 John Armstrong acquires Kenyon's way station, formerly known as Berings' on Pine Ridge, at today's Shaver Ranch site.

1905 Forest Reserves organized under U.S. Forest Service, Department of Agriculture; Sierra Preserve acreage increased to over 5 million acres.

1907 C. B. Shaver dies. Sierra National Forest established with 6.6 million acres.

1908 Sierra National Forest divided into Sequoia, Stanislaus, Mono and Inyo national forests, leaving Sierra with 1.9 million acres.

1909 Wagon road extended north from Shaver millpond to Manzanita Park, now known as Big Creek.

1910 Work begins on Big Creek hydroelectric project.

1912 Shaver sawmill sold to Ira Bennett, renamed Fresno Flume and Lumber Company of Nevada.

1914-15 Heavy winter destroys sections of Shaver-Clovis flume; under-capitalized and unable to rebuild, mill closes. Pacific Power and Light Company surveys a new and larger Shaver Lake.

1917 Pacific Light and Power Company merges with Southern California Edison Company.

1919 SCE purchases Shaver mill properties, reopens sawmill to produce lumber for Huntington-Florence dam projects. Lena Shaver establishes Rock Haven, first leisure-time subdivision. Mono Indians make their final mountain migration.

1922 County begins construction of new road up Tollhouse grade—now known as the "old" Tollhouse Road.

1923-25 Ockenden resort burns during the winter.

1925 SCE begins construction of Shaver dam by extending San Joaquin & Eastern Railroad from Dawn to Shaver.

1927 Shaver sawmill, fishing club and other buildings burned to clear new lake bed.

1928 New, enlarged Shaver Lake begins filling. John Harshman arrives, eventually becoming resort operator, postmaster and Shaver Lake developer.

1930 Fresno County develops campground on Shaver Lake Point.

1933 W. R. Miles makes first attempts at snow removal on county road to Shaver Lake. Forest Service uses Civilian Conservation Corps to combat blister rust infestation. Fresno-Shaver Lake county road added to state highway system as Route 168.

1935 The dark ages end as electricity arrives at Shaver Lake Heights.

1938 John Hodgkins sets up ski tow on Shaver Lake Point.

1939 Lena Shaver, widow of pioneer timberman, dies at Fresno.

1942 World War II soldiers guard Shaver Lake dam from potential saboteurs.

1945-46 World War II and gas rationing end, bringing first wave of Shaver Lake development as rest and recreation center.

1957 Highway 168 realigned above Shaver Lake. Snow removal upgraded with new maintenance station; year-round access of Shaver assured; permanent population starts to grow; China Peak ski area developed by Knute Flint.

1963 Construction begins on four-lane section of Highway 168, bypassing Tollhouse Road.

1964 Joe Wierick takes over bankrupt China Peak. Shaver Lake becomes major year-round recreation area.

1974 Helms hydroelectric project brings new growth to Shaver Lake area. Condos and subdivisions multiply.

1975 U.S. Forest Service relocates Pineridge district office from Big Creek to Shaver Lake.

1983 Balsam Meadows project begins, capturing hydroelectric potential from available head of Huntington-Shaver tunnel.

Suggested Reading

Additional insight into the history of Shaver Lake and Pine Ridge can be gained with the following books:

A Sawmill History of the Sierra National Forest, 1852-1940 by Burt Hurt. U.S. Forest Service, 1941.

Cultural Resources Overview of the Southern Sierra Nevada by Theodoratus Cultural Resources, Inc. and Archaeological Consulting and Research Services, Inc. U.S. Forest Service, 1984.

Fresno County—The Pioneer Years: From the Beginning to 1900 by Charles Clough and William Secrest, Jr. Panorama West Books, 1984.

Iron Men and Copper Wires by William A. Myers. Trans-Anglo, 1984.

Imperial Fresno. 1897. Reprint by Fresno City and County Historical Society, 1976.

History of the Sierra Nevada by Francis P. Farquhar. University of California Press, 1969.

Just Around Home at Auberry by Louis Kientz. 1983.

Meadow Lakes by Georgia Waltz. Sierra Printing and Lithography Company, 1967.

The History of Fresno County by Paul Vandor. Historic Records Company, 1919.

The Story of Big Creek by David H. Redinger. Angelus Press, 1949. Reissued and revised, 1987.

The Whistle Blows No More by Hank Johnston. Trans-Anglo, 1984.

Vintage Fresno by Edwin Eaton. Huntington Press, 1965.

Index